Easy Machine Paper Piecing

65 Quilt Blocks for Foundation Piecing

CAROL DOAK

That Patchwork Place®

Credits

Editor-in-Chief ....Barbara Weiland
Technical Editor ....Ursula Reikes
Managing Editor ....Greg Sharp
Copy Editor ....Liz McGehee
Text and Cover Design ....Joanne Lauterjung
Typesetting ....Joanne Lauterjung
Photography ....Brent Kane
Illustration and Graphics ....Laurel Strand

Easy Machine Paper Piecing©
© 1994 by Carol Doak
That Patchwork Place, Inc., PO Box 118, Bothell, WA 98041-0118 USA

Printed in the United States of America
99 98 97 96 95 94   6 5 4 3 2 1

Library of Congress Cataloging-in-Publication Data

Doak, Carol
      Easy machine paper piecing : 65 quilt blocks for foundation picing / Carol Doak.
          p.   cm.
      ISBN 1-56477-038-9 :
      1. Patchwork—Patterns. 2. Machine quilting—Patterns. I. Title.
TT835.D62   1994
746.9'7—dc20   93-28648
                                          CIP

Dedication

To my husband, Alan, for his love and support, and for being my best friend.

Acknowledgments

My heartfelt thanks and appreciation go to:

Sherry Reis, Pam Ludwig, Peggy Forand, Beth Meek, Doreen C. Burbank, Ginny Guaraldi, Moira Clegg, Mary Kay Sieve, Carolyn Inglis, Shawn Levy, and Nancy Bell for sharing their wonderful paper-pieced quilt projects and for their support and friendship;

Sandra Hatch, for her faith, counsel, and encouragement to go for it;

Terry Maddox, Barbara Wysocki, Carter Houck, Karen O'Dowd, Winsome Coutts, and Susan Raban for their support and for making quiltmaking a wonderful sharing art form;

The Covered Bridge Quilt Shop, Nashua, New Hampshire, for providing a delightful warm place to teach quiltmaking techniques; and to my quilting students for making teaching such a joy.

Barbara Weiland, Ursula Reikes, and the entire staff at That Patchwork Place for their support, expertise, and for their genuine caring to create the best book from my manuscript. I always found a helpful and cheerful voice on the telephone, and they all made the experience of writing this book a pleasure.

And finally to my husband, Alan, for his support, friendship, and for always being there with his wonderful computer expertise as I wrestled with the wonder and frustration of it all.

Contents

Preface

Paper piecing is not a new idea. Early quiltmakers pieced their scraps of fabric to paper in random fashion because the paper provided stability. Designs sewn in a straight-seam sequence are as old as the traditional Log Cabin block. Quiltmakers took this idea a step further when they drew the sewing lines on the wrong side of the paper, placed the fabric pieces right sides together on the front of the paper, then sewed from the wrong side of the paper. This technique provided stability to the fabric and accuracy in the piecing.

This book combines both of these concepts. Traditional patchwork blocks that are sewn in a straight-seam sequence were my primer. Then I began to create adaptations and variations of these designs. Through the use of the computer, I was able to draw the designs in quilt settings with different color schemes and see the wonderful patchwork possibilities these designs offered. One design led to another until I had a compilation of over one hundred and sixty designs. I soon realized it was time to stop making designs and smell the roses. This book contains some of my favorite designs, and I invite you to stop and smell the roses with me.

Introduction

I am always asking "Why?" Why do something one way rather than another? Why is a particular procedure the best way to accomplish the task? Why would you want to know more about blocks made with machine paper piecing?

- They are easy to make and do not require a high degree of skill. If you can sew a straight line on a machine, you can create accurate patchwork blocks.
- They are quick! There is no need to make templates for the patchwork shapes. There is no need to mark and precut the fabric to the exact patchwork shape and size.
- They provide a stable base that allows you to include fabrics which are not normally utilized in patchwork, such as lamés and silks.
- They provide extreme accuracy even when piecing the tiniest of pieces and the sharpest of points!
- They are a great place to use all those "scrap" pieces of fabric you have been collecting.
- They are just plain fun to make!

The concept of piecing quilt blocks on paper foundations is a simple one. A design with a straight-seam sequence is drawn on paper. Fabric pieces cut the approximate size are placed in sequence on the unmarked side of the paper, and the lines are sewn from the marked side of the paper. After each seam is sewn, the excess fabric is trimmed in the seam allowance, and the piece is opened up. Once the project is complete, the paper is torn away from the stitching. No template making, no fabric marking, and no high degree of skill is needed to accurately piece blocks one right after the other. One of my students described this technique as akin to eating potato chips. Once you get started, it's hard to stop!

Since designing is one aspect of quiltmaking that I really enjoy, it was fun creating blocks that fit the paper-piecing criteria. You can use the 4" blocks presented in this book to create a variety of quilt projects. You can enlarge them to create bed-size projects and reduce them for use in miniature quilt projects. You can also incorporate these blocks into vests, jackets, totes, clothing, and home-decorating items.

The "Block and Quilt Design Possibilities" section, beginning on page 61, offers possible block variations, fabric considerations, and block-placement ideas to get those creative juices flowing.

The Gallery of Quilts, beginning on page 83, illustrates several quilt projects that use the block designs in a variety of sizes and styles. Most of the quilters who made these projects had never used this method before. They all agreed machine paper piecing was fun.

I hope you enjoy making these blocks and using this easy method to create wonderful quilts.

Block Designs

The 4" block designs are full size and ready to use. The numbers on the block designs indicate the piecing sequence. The seam between piece #1 and piece #2 is sewn first, and the other seams follow in sequence. Some of the block designs require a unit with one or two prepieced seams. Pieced units are identified on the block pattern with a "//" through the seam and are explained in greater detail on pages 12–13.

Reproducing Block Designs

Tracing

Place a piece of tracing paper on top of the 4" block design and secure with masking tape to keep paper from shifting while drawing. Using a mechanical pencil and a ruler, trace the lines, markings, and numbers. Make a separate tracing for each block.

Although tracing the blocks by hand takes more time than using the copy machine, it does offer advantages. The lines are easier to see during the design and sewing process, and the paper is easier to remove.

Photocopying

You can use a copy machine to reproduce the blocks; however, copy machines do produce copies with variances. Photocopying a 4" original block produces a block that is just a "hair" larger (less than 1%). The blocks will be ever so slightly off square. A perfect square has identical diagonal measurements from corner to corner. A photocopy has a variance of approximately 1/16". This variance is so slight and occurs over such a great distance that normally you cannot see it. However, for this reason (compounding the variance), it is not advisable to make a copy from a copy. The designs for each project should be made on the same machine from the original block. Different copy machines may produce copies with a different variance. Always be sure that the photocopied blocks are the correct size for the intended project.

Use a rotary cutter and plastic square ruler to trim photocopies 1/2" from the outside lines on all sides. You can use your nicked and dull rotary blades for this purpose.

Enlarging and Reducing Block Designs

The lure of changing the size of the original block led me to investigate the reducing and enlarging options on the copy machine. After much experimentation, I have come to the conclusion that all enlargements and reductions for a chosen design should be made from original patterns and on the same copy machine. You can reduce copies to 64% and enlarge them to 156%. The same variance applies to blocks that you enlarge and reduce. A 3" block is 75% of the original, a 5" block is 125% of the original, and a 6" block is 150% of the original. You cannot enlarge a block larger than 6", however, without making a copy from an enlarged copy, where the variance is already present. I don't recommend making copies of copies because the variance becomes greater with each generation of photocopies.

Just on the outside chance that math is not your thing, I want to let you know about a handy chart tool called a Proportional Scale. You align the size of the original on the inner wheel with the desired size of the reduction or enlargement on the outer wheel, and like magic, the percentage of reduction or enlargement appears in the window!

Symmetrical and Asymmetrical Blocks

The 4" block designs represent the wrong side of the block. In a symmetrical design, the fabric side of the block will be the same as the marked side of the block. In an asymmetrical design, the fabric side of the block will be the reverse of the marked side of the block. Use the block-front drawings and the color photographs to see how the blocks will appear from the front once they are pieced.

Symmetrical Candle Blocks

Wrong side   Right side

Asymmetrical House Blocks

Wrong side   Right side

Even though a design is symmetrical, the fabric placement can be asymmetrical. To reproduce the colors in a block-front drawing, simply indicate the color of the pieces on the blank side of the paper design to correspond with the finished color example. If you trace the blocks on tracing paper, the lines are easy to see. If you photocopy the blocks, the lines should be dark enough to see from the unmarked side when the paper is placed on a white surface. If not, simply place a light source beneath the block so the lines are more visible.

Symmetrical Fabric Placement

Notations on unmarked side of block   Finished front

Asymmetrical Fabric Placement

 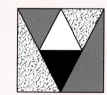

Notations on unmarked side of block   Finished front

Cutting Fabric Pieces to Approximate Size

To cut fabric the approximate size for the intended area, take a quick measurement of the area with a ruler and add a total of ¾" to 1". You will cut the pieces a bit larger than necessary, as the customary seam allowance for patchwork is ¼". You will trim the excess fabric to ¼" after you sew the adjoining seams. Since the line drawing that is being measured is the wrong side of the block, always cut the fabric with the *wrong side facing up*. You can fill in unusual shapes with oversize rectangles or squares. You don't need to cut the exact shape.

Remember, when dealing with angled seams and odd shapes, bigger is better. Before attaching these odd shapes, place the wrong side of the fabric on the blank side of the block, over the intended area. Hold the marked side of the foundation up to a light source and check to see that the cut piece of fabric is large enough to fill the intended area plus a ¼"-wide seam allowance all the way around. Since strips of fabric offer very little placement variance, I tend to cut them the finished size plus ½" for the seam allowances.

Fabric Grain Options

Fabric has three grains: lengthwise, crosswise, and bias. The lengthwise grain has the least amount of stretch and runs parallel to the selvages. The crosswise grain runs from selvage to selvage and has a bit of stretch. Both the lengthwise and the crosswise grains are considered the straight grain of the fabric. The bias runs diagonally through the fabric and has the greatest amount of stretch.

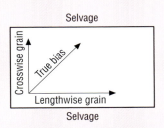

There are three choices as to fabric-grain placement when piecing on paper foundations. You can piece the blocks with random-grain placement, straight-grain placement, or a combination of both.

Random-Grain Placement

In this placement, fabric pieces are sewn with no attention paid to the direction of the fabric grain along the sewing edge. This results in random-grain direction when the piece is sewn and opened up. Paper piecing permits this type of random-grain piecing because the paper provides the stability necessary to prevent the pieces from stretching as they are sewn. However, bias edges along the edge of a block will stretch once the paper is removed. For this reason, I don't recommend using random-grain placement for block pieces that will fall at the outside edge of a project. It is also why I suggest that you do not remove the paper until the blocks have been joined to other blocks and/or borders.

Large pieces of fabric with random-grain placement can be distracting. Since fabric grain is more obvious in solid-colored fabrics, use tiny-scale prints in place of solid-colored fabrics to help camouflage random-grain directions.

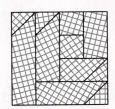

Random-grain placement

Straight-Grain Placement

Fabric pieces in this placement are sewn so the straight of grain is vertical and horizontal through the block. This placement is important for block pieces that will be used at the outside edges of a project and when the fabric pieces are large enough to make the fabric grain noticeable.

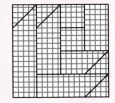

Straight-grain placement

Vertical and Horizontal Seam Lines

The Courthouse Steps block is an example of a block that contains only vertical and horizontal lines. All the fabric strips and the center square should be cut on the straight grain of the fabric and then placed on vertical and horizontal seam lines.

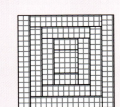

Straight-grain placement on vertical and horizontal lines

Diagonal Seam Lines

Fabrics that will be used on diagonal seam lines should be cut on the bias so that the vertical and horizontal sides of the block will both be on the straight grain of the fabric. In the block at right, the sewing edges of the pieces are all cut on the bias.

To cut fabric on the bias, cut strips diagonally at a 45° angle.

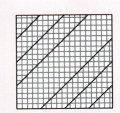

Bias-grain placement on diagonal lines

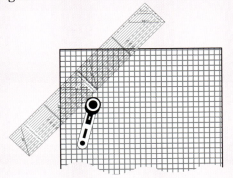

"Weird" Angle Seam Lines

"Weird"-grain fabric edges are placed on "weird" angles. I have designated any seam line as "weird" if it is not horizontal, vertical, or at a 45° angle. I use this term only because it is not necessary to know what the angle is, only how to cut the fabric so that it will end up on the straight grain once it is sewn and opened up. Use the following method to cut "weird" angles so they will finish on the straight of grain:

1. Place the block design on the cutting mat.
2. Place a long rotary ruler along the seam line you are about to sew—the "weird" angle.
3. Place the fabric you intend to use, wrong side up, either above or below the block and under the extending end of the ruler; cut the angle with a rotary cutter. Make sure the straight grain of the fabric runs vertically and horizontally.

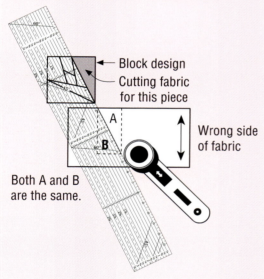

Block design

Cutting fabric for this piece

Wrong side of fabric

Both A and B are the same.

4. Cut "weird" angles as needed to avoid possible confusion. I like to make a small pencil mark on the paper block of the weird-angle line I just cut so I don't forget.
5. Place the cut edge of the fabric along the seam; sew in place and open up.

To cut the reverse of the same weird angle at the same time, fold the fabric right sides together and cut both layers at the same time. When cutting bias pieces and weird angles, bigger is better. Oversize cut pieces will ensure that the fabric will fill the intended area once it is sewn and opened up. You can always trim the excess fabric after sewing the adjoining pieces.

When the first piece of a block contains weird angles, simply pin the piece right side up with the straight grain going vertically and horizontally.

Fabric Strips

Several block designs utilize strips of fabric. Use straight-grain strips when the strips are set vertically or horizontally in the block. You can also use straight-grain strips along diagonal seams if you are piecing with random-grain placement. Cut bias strips for diagonally placed strips so that edges will finish on the straight of grain.

You can precut a supply of fabric strips on the bias or on the straight of grain to the finished width plus ½" for seam allowances. Add straight-grain fabric strips to any of the paper block designs to enlarge them or to stabilize the outside edges where you have used random-grain fabric placement.

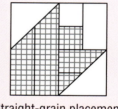

Straight-grain placement

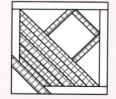

Random-grain placement

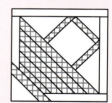

Bias strips for straight-grain placement at edges of block

You have probably just read more about fabric grain than you ever wanted to know. Don't become overwhelmed. Deal with it on a block-by-block basis at first, and it will become second nature.

Quilt Blocks

This chapter contains the "nuts and bolts" of machine paper piecing blocks. There is much more information presented than you need to get started. Since the best way to learn is through doing, begin by piecing small blocks with random-grain placement to practice the mechanics. Then, move on to the larger blocks and straight-grain placement. As you create the blocks, the techniques will become second nature. Of course, if you need a refresher, you can always refer to this "nuts and bolts" chapter.

Getting Ready to Sew

Whenever I begin a project, I set the stage so that I have everything I am going to need at my fingertips. Jumping up for this or that may burn calories, but it cuts down on the speed and the fun you are about to have.

- Make sure that your sewing machine is in good working order and sews a good straight stitch.
- Set the stitch length on the machine for approximately 18 to 20 stitches per inch. A short stitch length perforates the paper better, which makes it easier to tear away later.
- Use a size 90/14 needle; the larger needle also helps perforate the paper.
- Select a sewing thread that blends with most of the fabrics used.
- Create a pressing and cutting area next to the machine by lowering the ironing board down to sewing level; use one end to cut and the other end to press.
- Have a sharp pair of small scissors handy to trim the fabric pieces before and after they are sewn.
- Have your rotary cutter, plastic ruler, and mat close at hand. Choose the ruler size based upon the size of the blocks being made.
- Have your "unsewing" tool (seam ripper) handy just on the outside chance that a quick take-out maneuver becomes necessary.
- Set up a small lamp near the sewing machine. Generally, the fabric placement of the first piece is easy to see without a light source. However, to place subsequent pieces of fabric, you need to be able to see through the previous pieces of untrimmed fabric.

- Last, but probably most important, select your fabric. Remember, the unmarked side of the block is the fabric side. To avoid any confusion, always note your fabric choices on the unmarked side of the block design.

⭐ **TIP:** When using larger pieces of fabric (rather than scraps), cut strips approximately 6" wide; then, cut smaller pieces from the strips as needed. This makes the fabric more manageable and the sewing area less cluttered.

Now you are all set to begin piecing. You might want to put on some relaxing music and make yourself a cup of tea. This is going to be fun!

Step-By-Step Sewing Procedure

1. Place the fabric for piece #1, right side up, on the unmarked side of the paper; pin in place. Make sure piece #1 covers the area marked 1 and extends at least ¼" on all sides. You can cut the piece larger than needed and trim the excess fabric after the adjoining seams are sewn. Once you have sewn a few blocks, you may want to just hold the first piece in position and eliminate the pin. If copy paper is used, hold the paper up to a light source with the marked side of the block toward you, to facilitate proper placement.

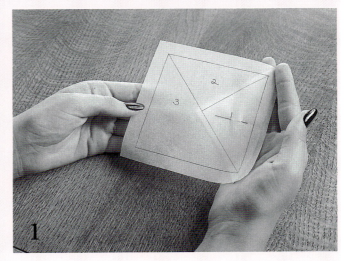

2. With the wrong side of the fabric facing you, cut the approximate size piece #2. Remember, the marked side of the block is the wrong side of the block.

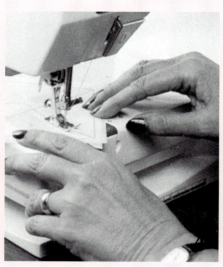

3. Place piece #2 on top of piece #1, right sides together, along the joining seam line; make sure both fabrics extend by at least ¼" beyond the seam lines. Don't concern yourself with an exact ¼"-wide seam allowance. You can trim any excess seam allowance after the seam is sewn. However, you do want to keep the edge of piece #2 parallel to the seam line to keep the grain true.

★ **TIP:** Check to make sure the piece is placed correctly and is large enough by pinching the seam-allowance edge and opening up piece #2 to see if it covers the intended area plus seam allowances.

4. Holding the fabrics in place, lay the paper block with the marked side up under the presser foot and sew the first seam line between pieces #1 and #2.

Extend the stitching a few stitches beyond the beginning and the end of the line.

5. Trim away any excess fabric in the seam allowance to ¼". Open up piece #2 and finger press by running your fingers across the seam. Press with an iron on a cotton setting with no steam.

6. Add piece #3 across the first two. Sew the second seam line between pieces #1/#2 and piece #3.

7. Using a rotary cutter and ruler, trim the edges of the block, leaving a ¼"-wide seam allowance beyond the outside lines of the marked design. If the ruler slips on the paper, apply small, circular stick-on tabs of sandpaper to stabilize it.

No matter how many pieces a block design has, the construction is the same. Always add pieces in numerical order until the design is complete.

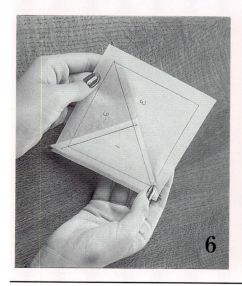

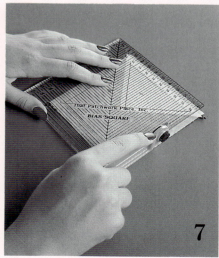

Finished Block

Sewing Tips

- Whenever possible, stitch in the direction of the points. This makes it easy to see that you are crossing the other line of stitching at the desired location.

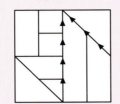

Stitch in the direction
of points when possible.

- Use an open-front presser foot on your machine for the best visibility.

- If you need several half-square triangles, cut over-size squares (finished short side of the triangle plus 1¼") and cut once diagonally.

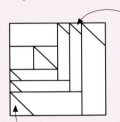

Finished size: ½"
Cut 2 squares 1¾" x 1¾" to yield
4 half-square triangles.

Finished size: 1"
Cut 1 square 2¼" x 2¼" to yield
2 half-square triangles.

- If you need several quarter-square triangles, cut oversize squares (finished long side of the triangle plus 1½") and cut twice diagonally.

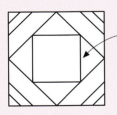

Finished size: 2"
Cut 1 square 3½" x 3½"
and cut twice diagonally to yield
4 quarter-square triangles.

- When trimming seam allowances, fold the paper back slightly so it will not interfere.
- Use tissue-paper tracings when you want to center a design on the first piece of fabric you are placing. The design is easier to see through tissue paper.

- Hold the paper on both sides while sewing for better control.
- When adding straight-grain strips to the outside of several blocks that will be joined, alternate the long pieces from the top and bottom edges to the sides so you won't have to match seam intersections.

- You can finger press each seam to quickly crease the pieces when your iron is not close at hand.
- Always overestimate the size of the pieces; you can always trim away the excess. Remember, bigger is better!
- Since it is difficult to see if you are sewing striped or checked fabrics straight from the reverse side, you may want to choose fabrics that do not have a directional print.
- In areas where lots of seams come together, consider using a dark fabric to cover the seam allowances.
- If you open the fabric and the piece doesn't quite meet at a perfect point, simply take a deeper seam.
- Cut the excess threads after you sew each seam.
- If the project calls for multiple blocks in identical fabrics, make one block to confirm your fabric choices; then make the remainder of the blocks in assembly-line fashion, adding the same piece to each block before adding the next piece.
- If you can't trim the seam allowances to ¼" because of cross-seam stitching, simply lift the seam to pull the stitching away from the paper.
- Consider using the wrong side of the fabric as the right side. Often, it will appear as a lighter-colored version of the print.
- Iron delicate fabrics, such as lamés and silks, by pressing from the paper side once the piece has been opened up. If you are using copies from a copy machine, protect your iron from the ink, which may transfer onto a hot iron, by using a scrap pressing cloth.

Pieced Units

Adding pieced units expands the design possibilities. A pieced unit is noted by a "//" mark through the prepieced seam, and the unit is assigned a number in the sequence.

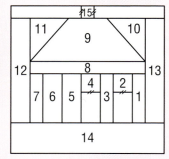

Single Straight-Seam Units

The House block is used as an example to show how the windows are prepieced to make one unit. To determine the size of the fabric strips needed, measure the height of the window and add at least ½" for seam allowances. The windows in the example measure ½" wide, so cut a 1"-wide strip. Measure the height of the house section and add at least ½" for seam allowances. The house section in the example is $^{13}/_{16}$"; cut a $1^5/_{16}$" strip of house fabric. Remember, this is the minimum width since you can cut the strips wider and trim the excess fabric after you add the pieced unit in sequence. Cut the strips long enough for the number of units needed. Sew the two strips together, measure the width of the window, add ½", and cut the strip into the required-size units. In this example, cut units at least 1" wide. Position the pieced unit in place, aligning the seam along the marked (//) seam line. Remember, you can always trim away excess fabric, so you can cut single-seam prepieced units larger than necessary.

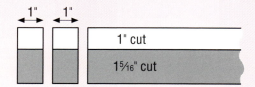

Single Bias-Seam Units

The Cat block requires a pieced unit with a 45°-angle seam. Measure the length and width of the upper and lower pieces. Cut a strip for each piece ½" larger than the width and 1½" longer than the length. Place the 45° line of a rotary ruler on the long edge of the wrong side of the fabric strip and cut the end on the angle as shown.

CAUTION: Have the block design at hand so you can be sure you are cutting the line in the same direction. When both strips have been cut, join them right sides together with a ¼"-wide seam allowance. Press seam toward the darker fabric.

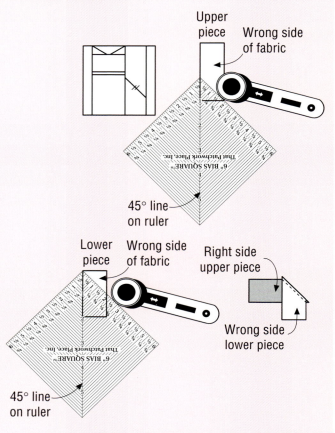

To ensure accurate placement of the angled seam, place a straight pin ¼" from the edge of the pieced unit at the seam; then place the point of the pin through the paper into the exact place where the seam should be joined; pin in place before sewing.

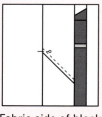

Fabric side of block

The following Geometric block requires a corner unit that is pieced with the straight grain falling on the corners. Cut a square from each fabric the finished size of the long side of triangle A or B plus 1½"; then cut the two squares twice diagonally into eight quarter-square triangles. You will use only four triangles for each block. Prepiece two quarter-square triangles together as shown to make this prepieced A/B unit.

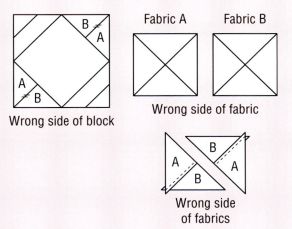

Wrong side of block

Fabric A   Fabric B

Wrong side of fabric

Wrong side
of fabrics

When making several blocks, cut the strips the correct width and long enough to accommodate the number of units needed. For example, the bottom strip of the Tree block is 1" finished; add ½" for seam allowances. If you need ten units, multiply 1½" x 10 and cut each strip 15" long. Cut 1 strip for the trunk, 1¼" x 15"; cut 2 strips for the background, each 2⅛" x 15". Sew the trunk strip between 2 background strips; then cut the strip set into 1½"-wide units and attach to the bottom of the blocks.

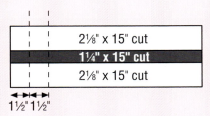

2⅛" x 15" cut
1¼" x 15" cut
2⅛" x 15" cut

1½" 1½"

Double Straight-Seam Units

Several of the Tree blocks and House blocks require a pieced unit with two straight seams. The Tree block is used as an example; however, the same information holds true for the chimney section in the House blocks. If making only one unit, cut the trunk strip the finished measurement plus ½" for seam allowances. Cut two pieces of background fabric the finished measurement plus ½" for seam allowances. Piece the three pieces together with the trunk fabric in the center; join to the bottom of the tree as one unit, aligning the seam lines with the drawing.

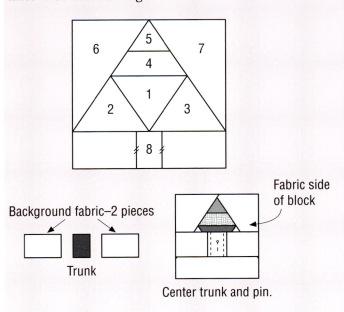

Background fabric–2 pieces

Trunk

Fabric side
of block

Center trunk and pin.

Block Designs

The designs are grouped into the following six categories:

Geometric	G1–G18
Flowers	F1–F14
Baskets	B1–B8
Hearts	H1–H7
Trees	T1–T7
Pictures	P1–P11

Rather than name each of the block designs as is normally the case in patchwork, I have assigned letters and numbers for reference purposes.

Block Photos

These blocks are only suggestions for fabric placement in a finished block. There are many other options that will yield different patchwork varieties from the same line drawing. Blocks include ¼"-wide seam allowances.

4" Block Designs

You can trace, photocopy, enlarge, or reduce the block designs to create quilt blocks. The lines on the block design represent the sewing lines, and the numbers represent the piecing sequence. Using paper piecing to make blocks is quick; however, a block with five pieces is still quicker to piece than a block with seventeen pieces.

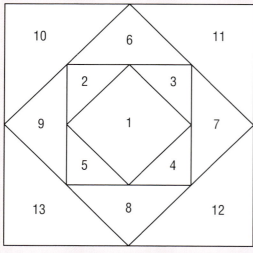

4" Block Design (stitching side)

The 4" block design represents the wrong side of the block. This is of no consequence for symmetrical blocks with symmetrical fabric placement. However, asymmetrical blocks or asymmetrical fabric placement will result in the reverse pattern on the finished side.

Block designs that have several merging seams at one corner are shown with an optional seam variation, which is indicated with a dotted line. See page 61 for more information about added seam variations.

Block-Front Drawings

These small drawings show how the finished blocks will appear from the fabric side. They can be photocopied and used for quilt-design purposes. You can also make quilt layout work sheets (page 63) to help you create your own quilt layouts. Arrange the blocks in several settings and in conjunction with other blocks until you have created a pleasing design. Once satisfied with your layout, photocopy the design layout several times and use colored pencils to try out different color schemes. Always use the block-front drawings to make your design and color selection and note your choices on the unmarked side of the corresponding 4" block designs.

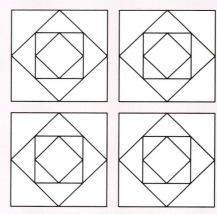

Block-Front Drawings

Geometric Blocks

G1
Color photo: page 31

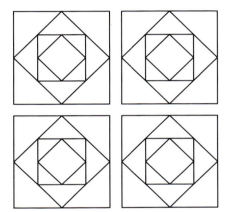

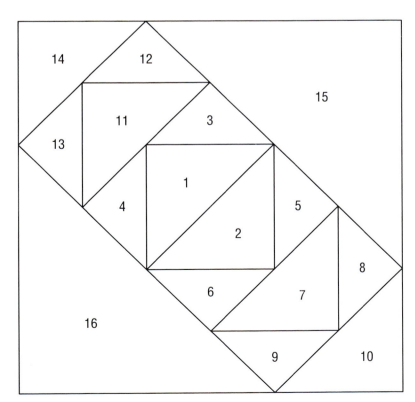

G2
Color photo: page 31

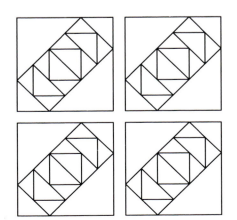

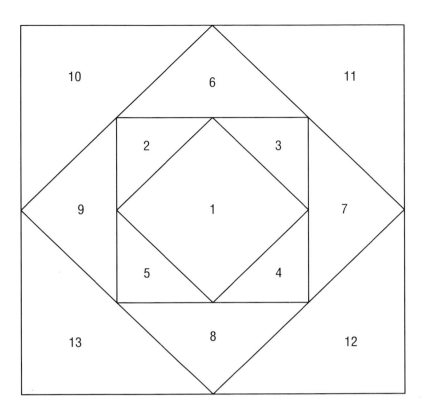

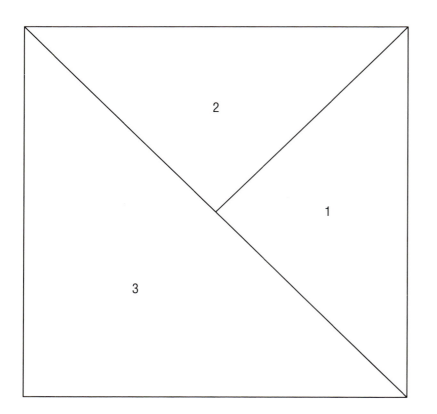

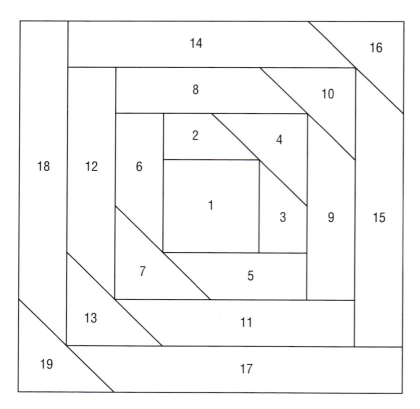

G3

Color photo: page 31

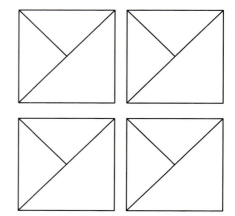

G4

Color photo: page 31

G5

Color photo: page 31

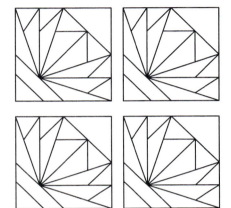

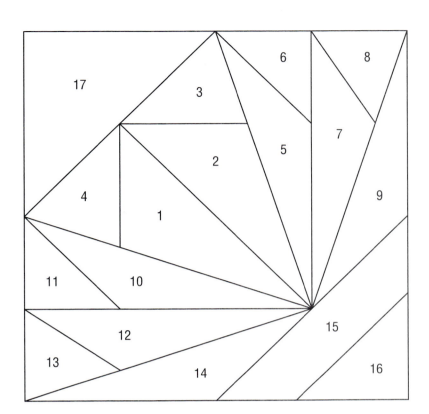

G6

Color photo: page 31

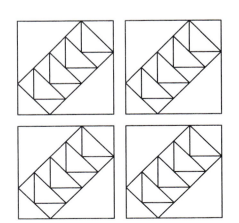

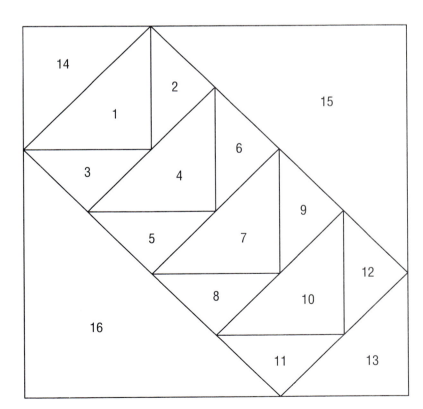

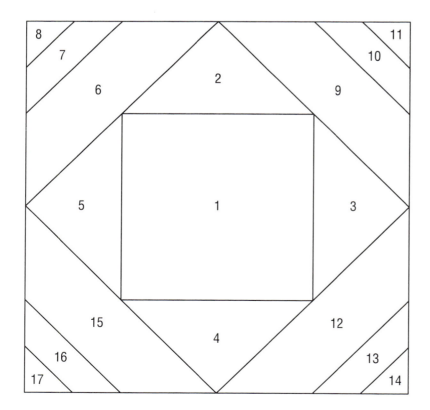

G7
Color photo: page 32

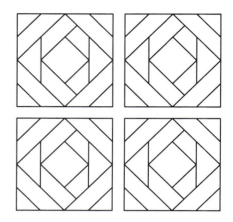

G8
Color photo: page 32

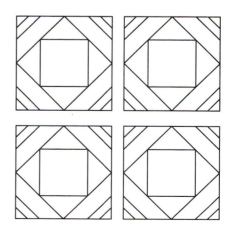

G9

Color photo: page 32

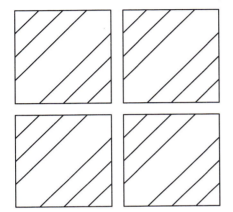

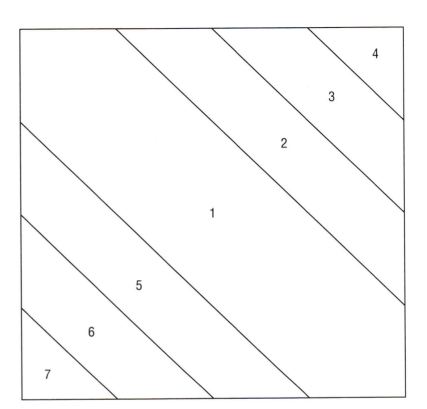

G10

Color photo: page 32

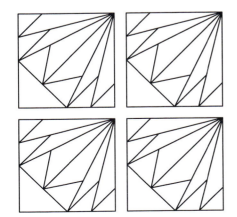

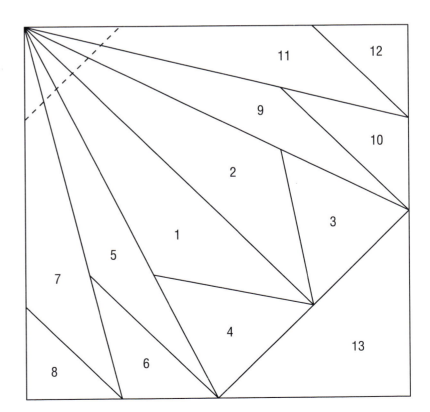

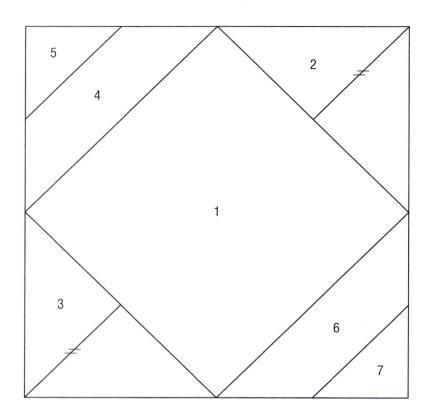

G11
Color photo: page 32

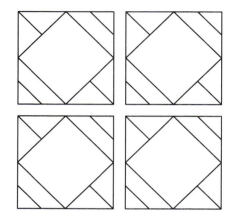

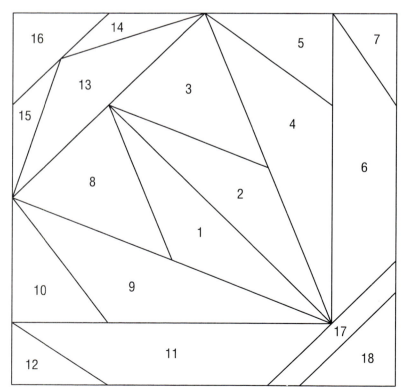

G12
Color photo: page 32

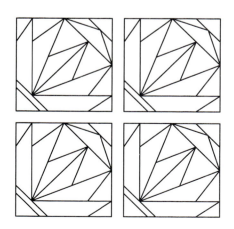

G13

Color photo: page 33

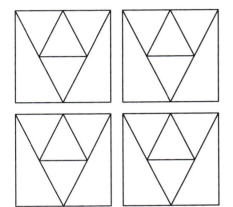

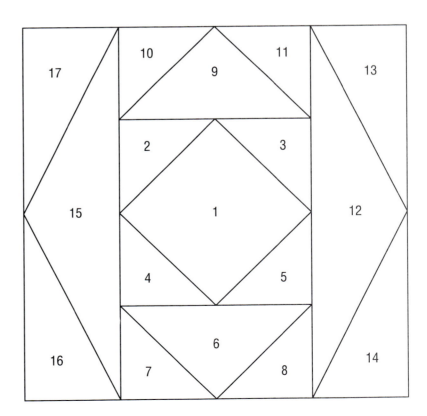

G14

Color photo: page 33

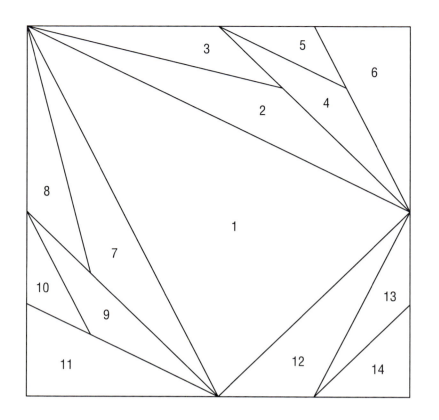

3

5

6

2

4

8

1

13

7

10

9

12

14

11

G15
Color photo: page 33

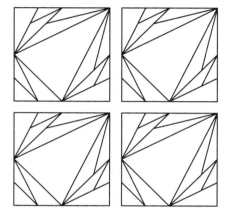

7

10   11

2   3

6   1   8

5   4

13   12

9

G16
Color photo: page 33

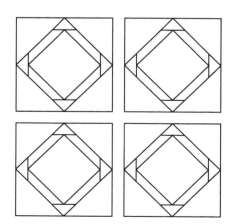

G17

Color photo: page 33

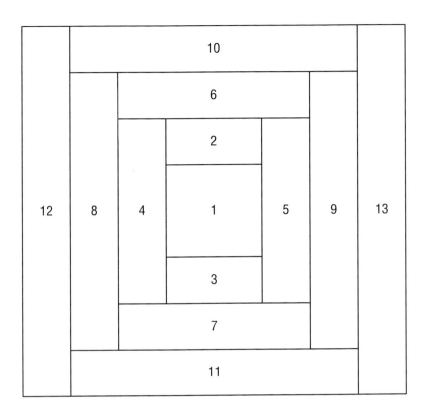

G18

Color photo: page 33

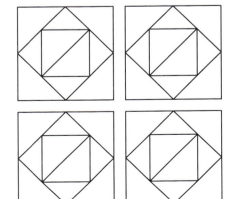

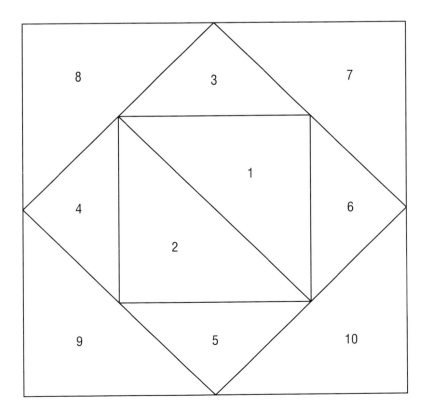

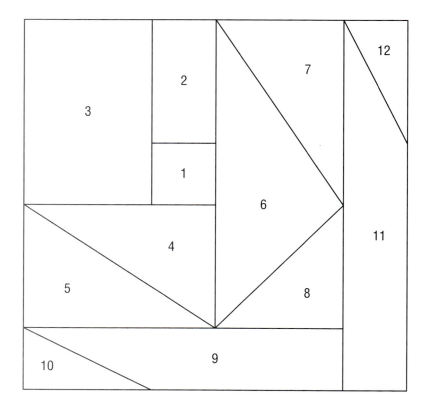

F1
Color photo: page 34

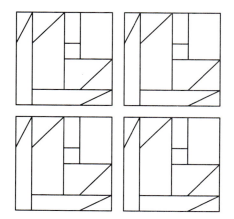

F2
Color photo: page 34

F3

Color photo: page 34

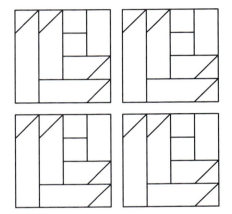

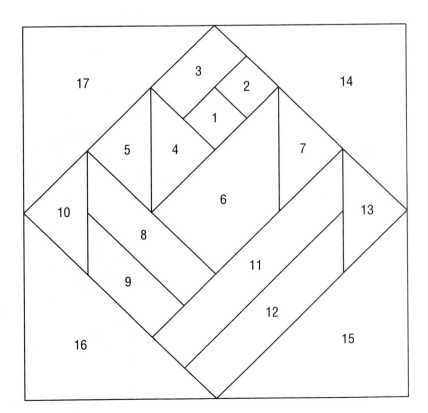

F4

Color photo: page 34

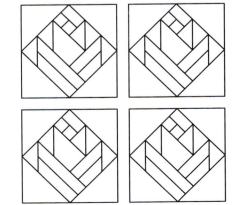

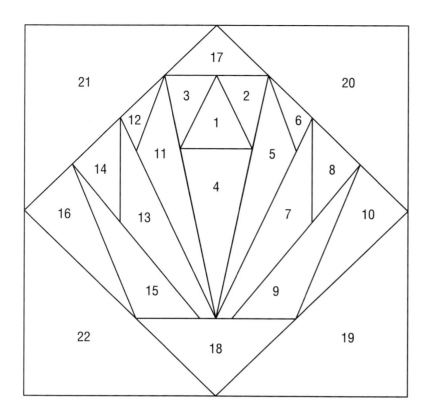

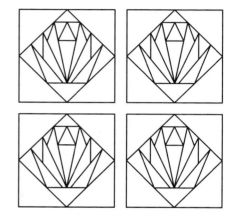

F5

Color photo: page 34

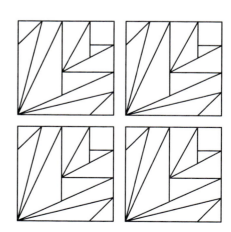

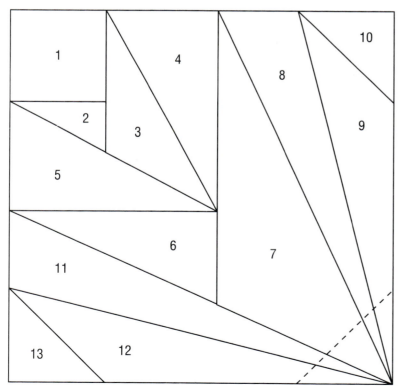

F6

Color photo: page 34

F7
Color photo: page 34

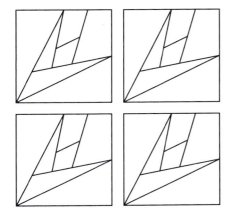

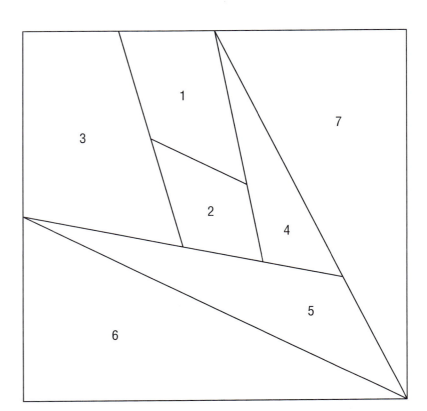

F8
Color photo: page 35

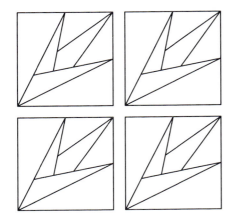

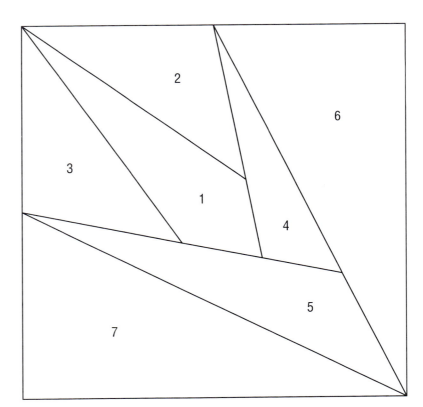

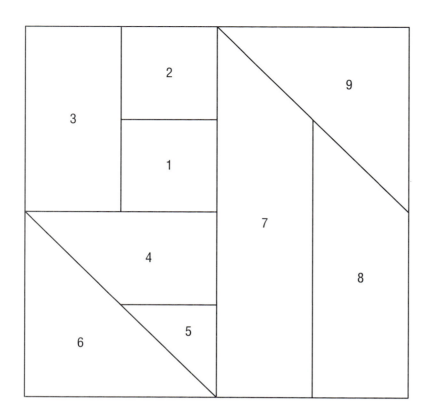

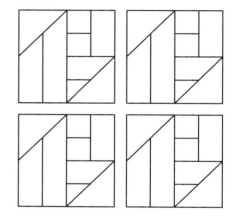

F9

Color photo: page 35

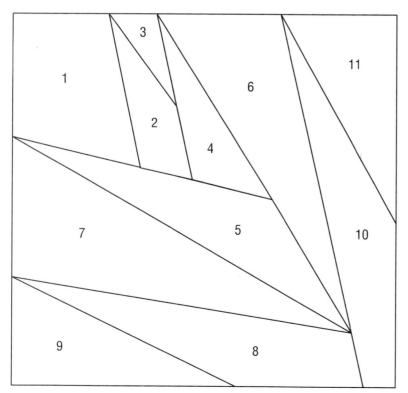

F10

Color photo: page 35

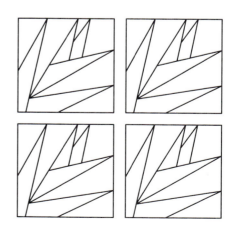

F11

Color photo: page 35

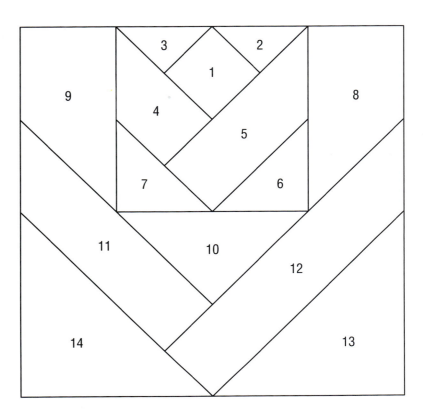

F12

Color photo: page 35

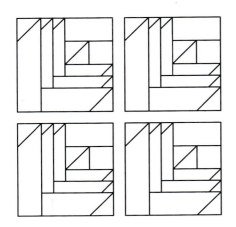

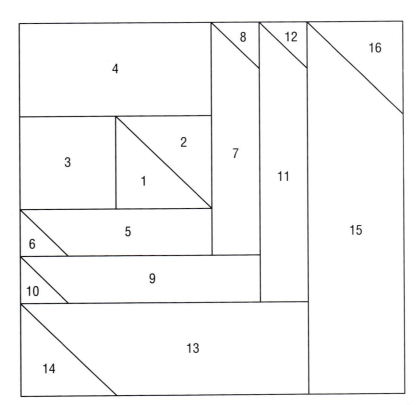

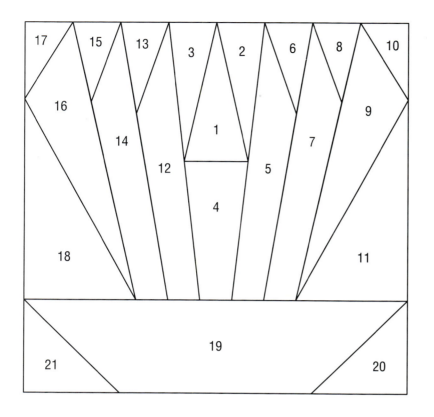

F13
Color photo: page 35

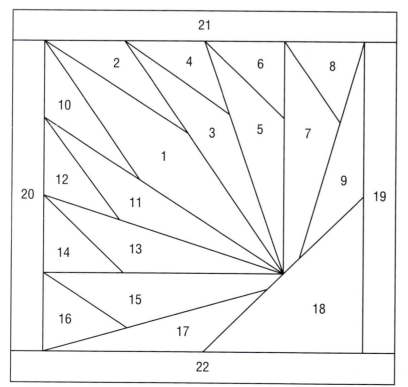

F14
Color photo: page 35

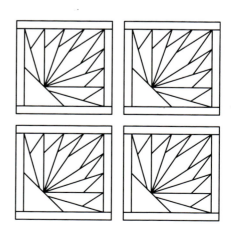

Geometric Blocks

G1
(page 15)

G2
(page 15)

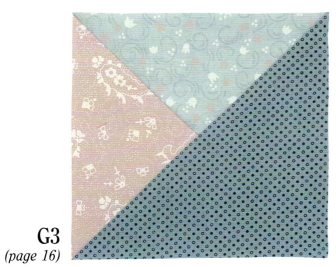

G3
(page 16)

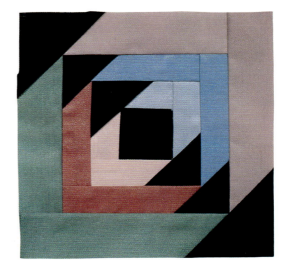

G4
(page 16)

G5
(page 17)

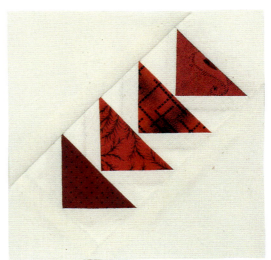

G6
(page 17)

G7
(page 18)

G8
(page 18)

G9
(page 19)

G10
(page 19)

G11
(page 20)

G12
(page 20)

G13
(page 21)

G14
(page 21)

G15
(page 22)

G16
(page 22)

G17
(page 23)

G18
(page 23)

Flower Blocks

F1
(page 24)

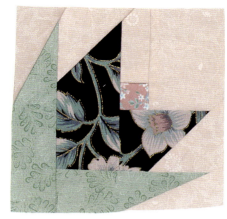

F2
(page 24)

F3
(page 25)

F4
(page 25)

F5
(page 26)

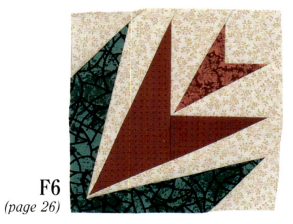

F6
(page 26)

F7
(page 27)

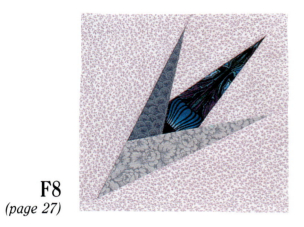

F8
(page 27)

F9
(page 28)

F10
(page 28)

F11
(page 29)

F12
(page 29)

F13
(page 30)

F14
(page 30)

Basket Blocks

B1
(page 37)

B2
(page 37)

B3
(page 38)

B4
(page 38)

B5
(page 39)

B6
(page 39)

B7
(page 40)

B8
(page 40)

Basket Blocks

B1

Color photo: page 36

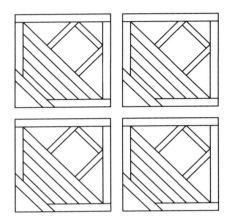

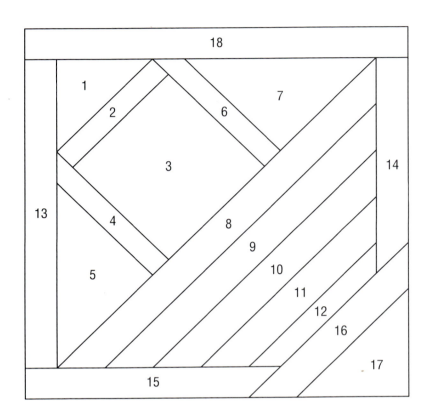

B2

Color photo: page 36

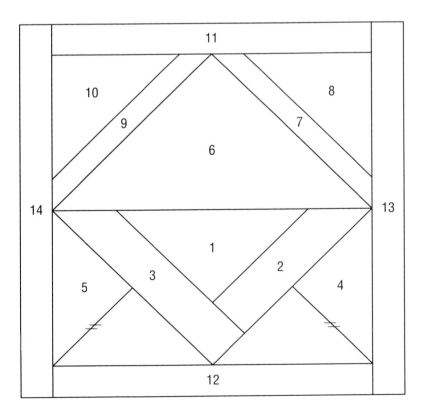

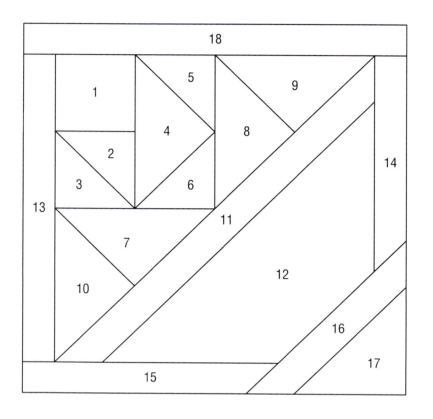

B3
Color photo: page 36

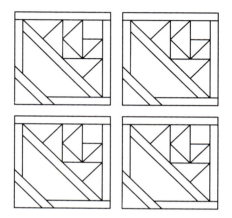

B4
Color photo: page 36

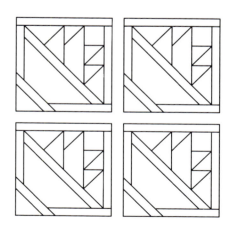

B5

Color photo: page 36

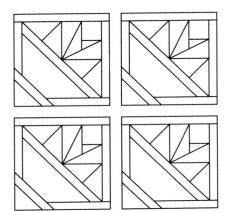

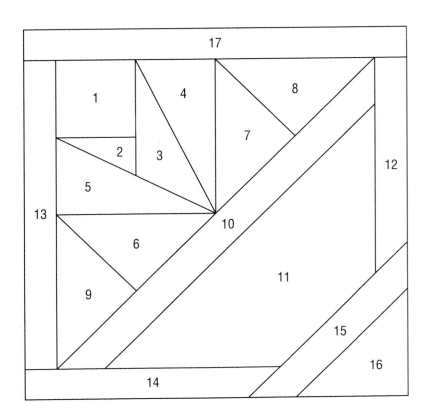

B6

Color photo: page 36

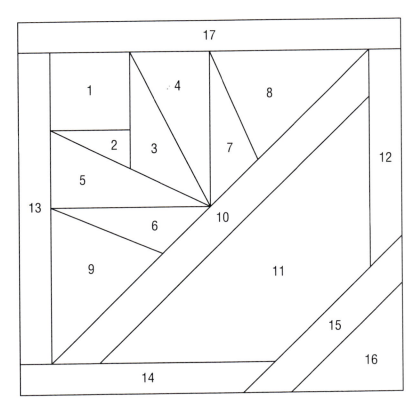

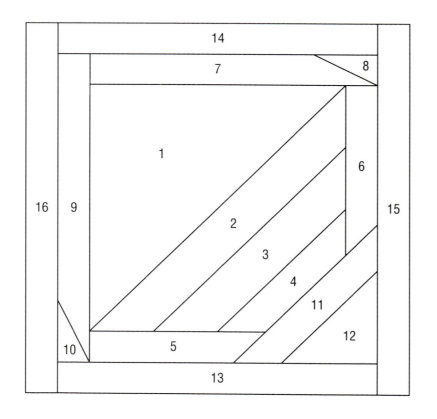

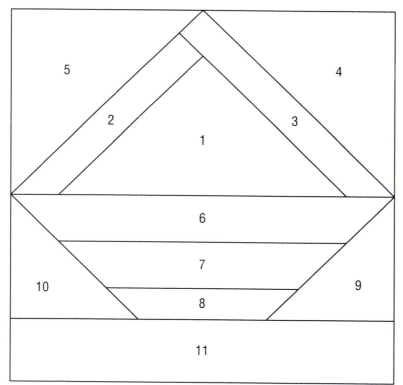

B7
Color photo: page 36

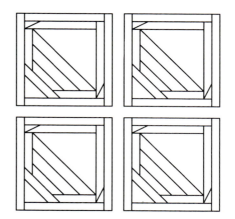

B8
Color photo: page 36

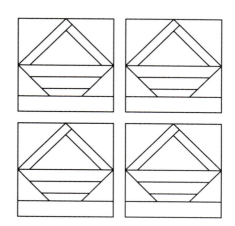

Heart Blocks

H1
Color photo: page 45

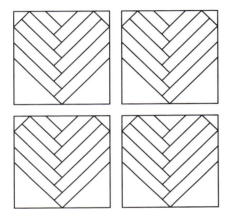

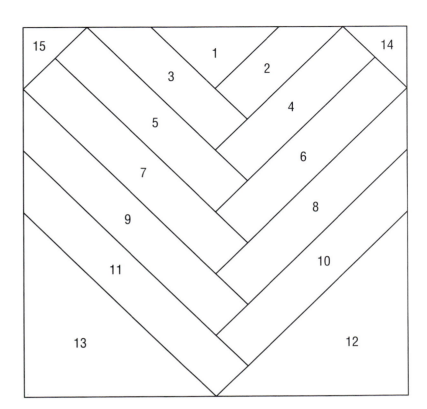

H2
Color photo: page 45

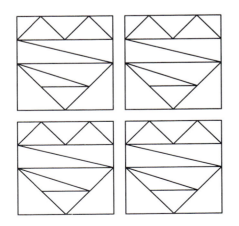

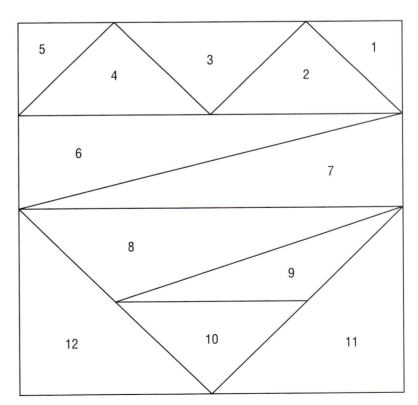

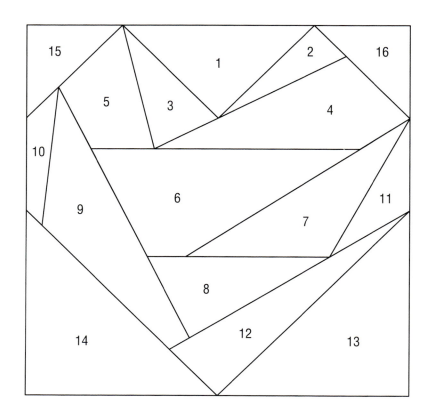

H3
Color photo: page 45

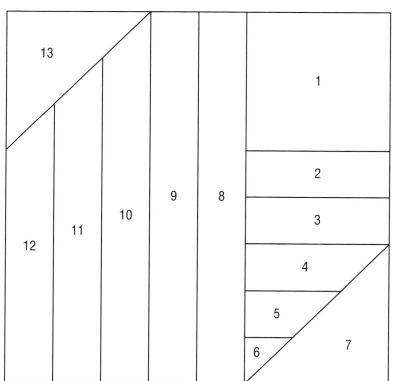

H4
Color photo: page 45

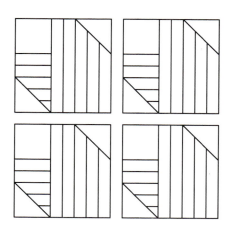

H5

Color photo: page 45

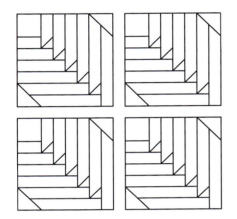

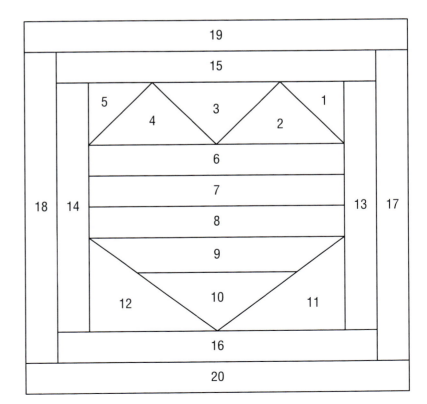

H6

Color photo: page 45

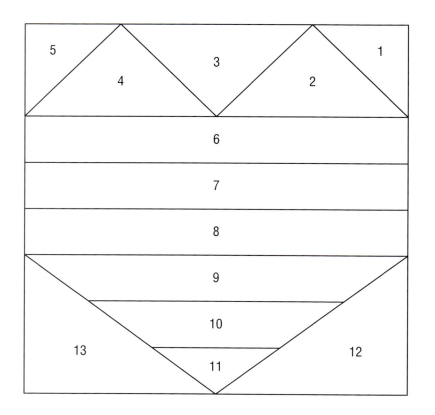

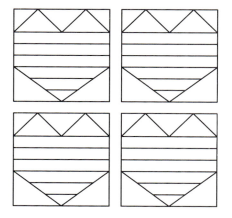

H7

Color photo: page 45

Heart Blocks

H1
(page 41)

H2
(page 41)

H3
(page 42)

H4
(page 42)

H5
(page 43)

H6
(page 43)

H7
(page 44)

Tree Blocks

T1
(page 49)

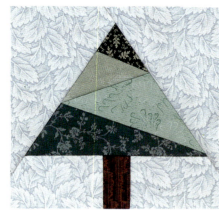

T2
(page 49)

T3
(page 50)

T4
(page 50)

T5
(page 51)

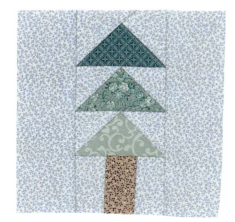

T6
(page 51)

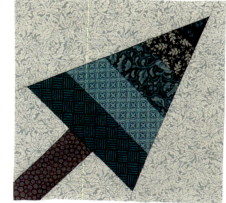

T7
(page 52)

Picture Blocks

P1
(page 52)

P2
(page 53)

P3
(page 53)

P4
(page 54)

P5
(page 54)

P6
(page 55)

P7
(page 55)

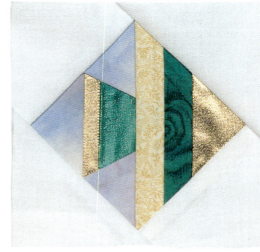

P8
(page 56)

P9
(page 56)

P10
(page 57)

P11 *(page 57)*

Tree Blocks

T1
Color photo: page 46

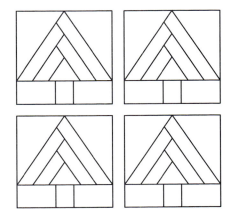

T2
Color photo: page 46

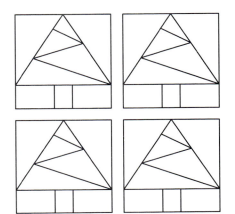

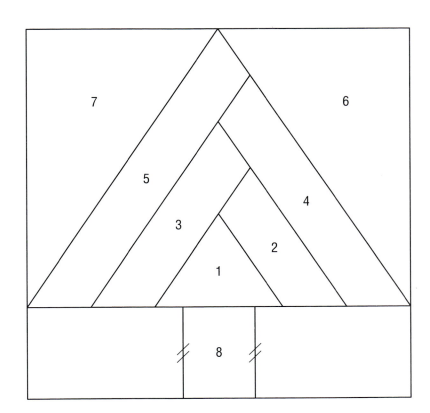

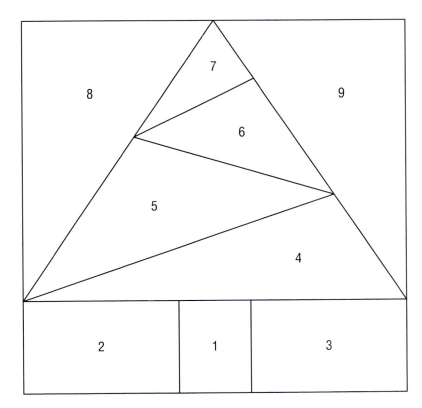

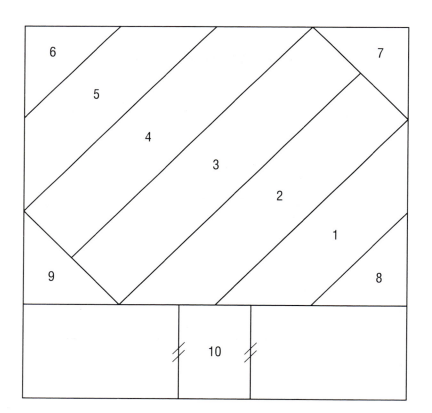

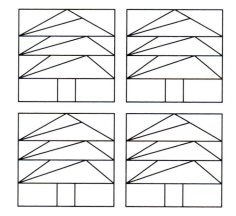

T3

Color photo: page 46

T4

Color photo: page 46

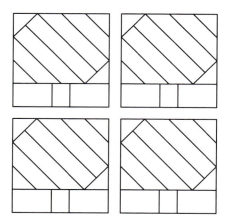

T5

Color photo: page 46

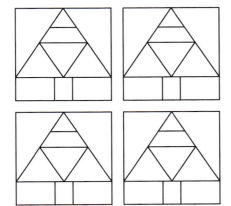

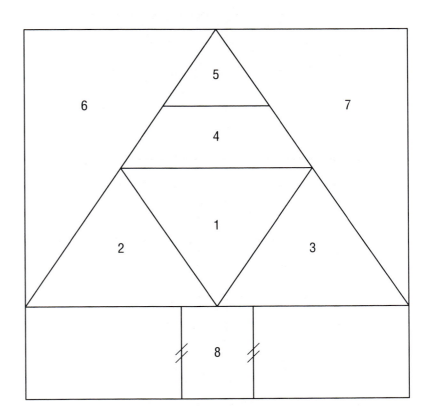

T6

Color photo: page 46

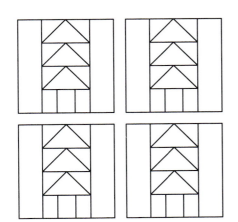

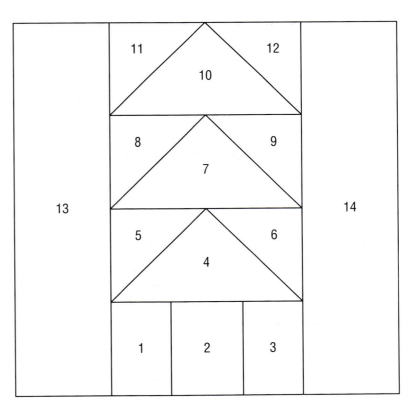

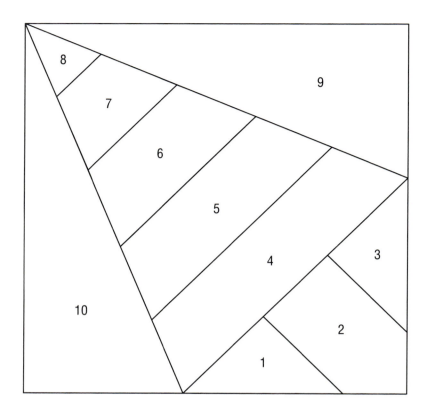

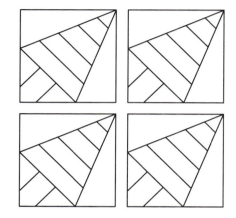

T7
Color photo: page 46

Picture Blocks

P1
Color photo: page 47

P2

Color photo: page 47

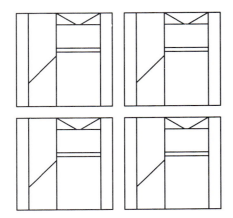

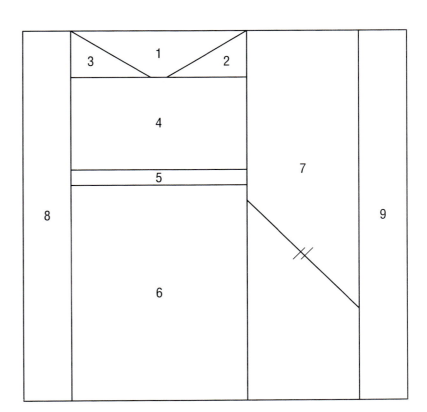

P3

Color photo: page 47

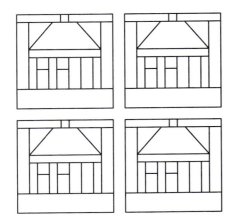

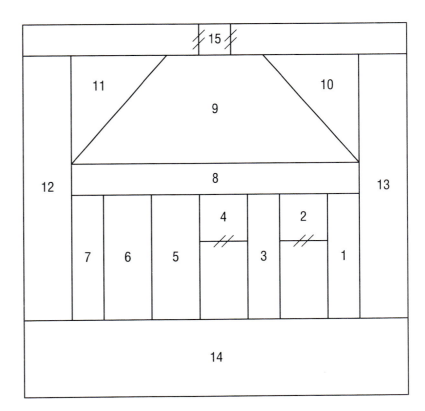

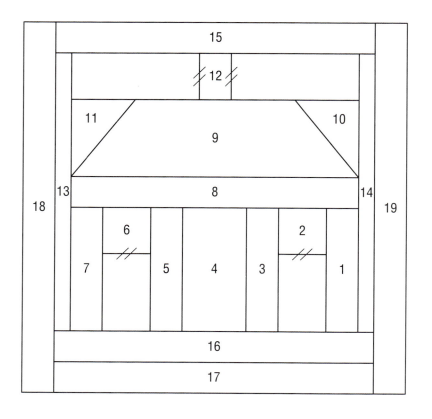

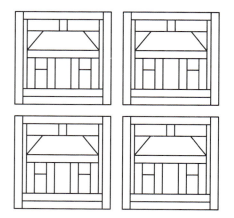

P4
Color photo: page 47

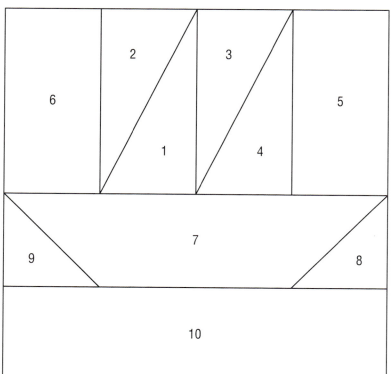

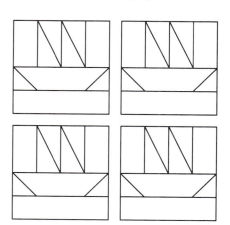

P5
Color photo: page 47

P6

Color photo: page 47

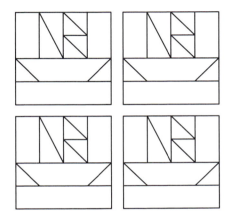

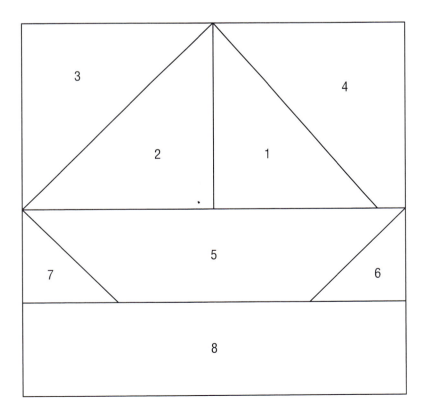

P7

Color photo: page 48

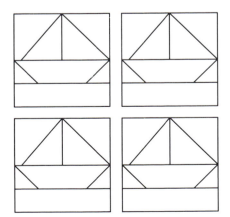

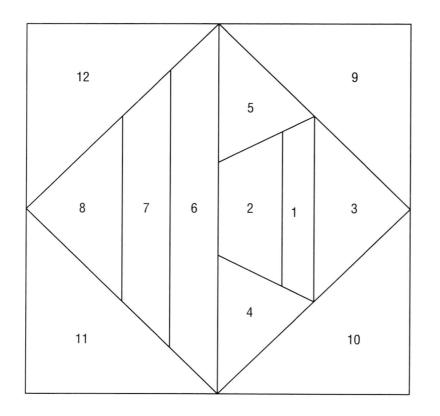

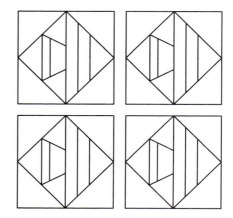

P8
Color photo: page 48

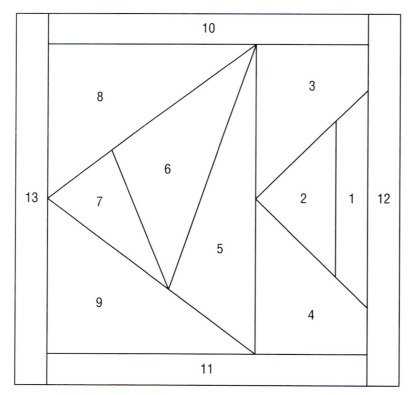

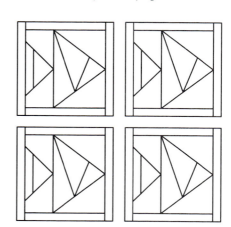

P9
Color photo: page 48

P10

Color photo: page 48

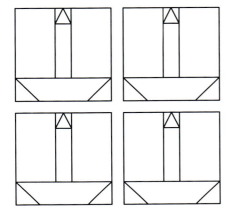

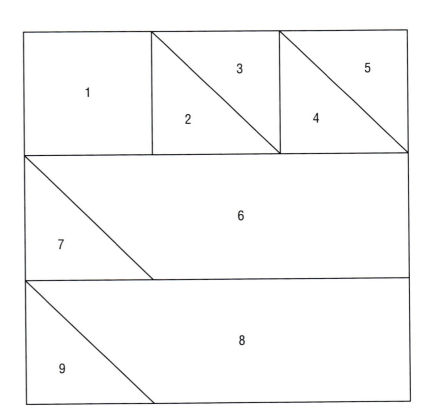

P11

Color photo: page 48

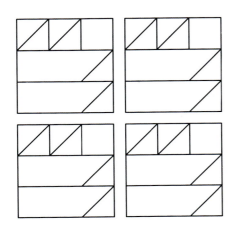

7" Block for G8 and G8 variation in the Not Exactly Amish quilt shown on page 79.

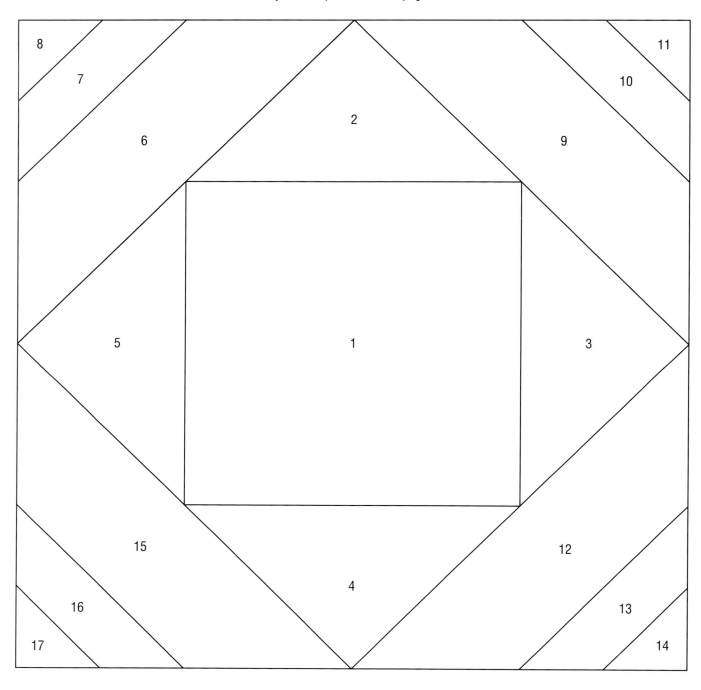

Block Designs

7" Block for F5 variation in the Tulip quilt shown on page 74.

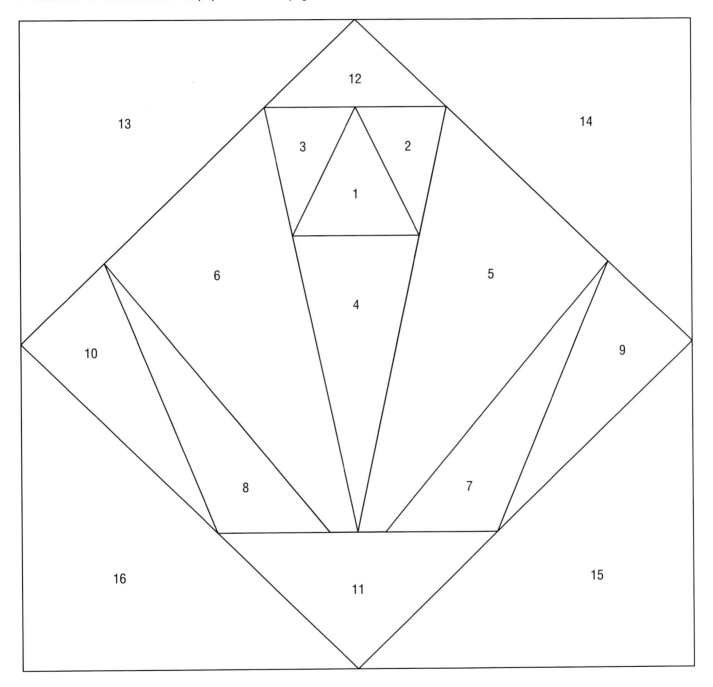

7" Block for F4 variation in the Tulip quilt shown on page 74.

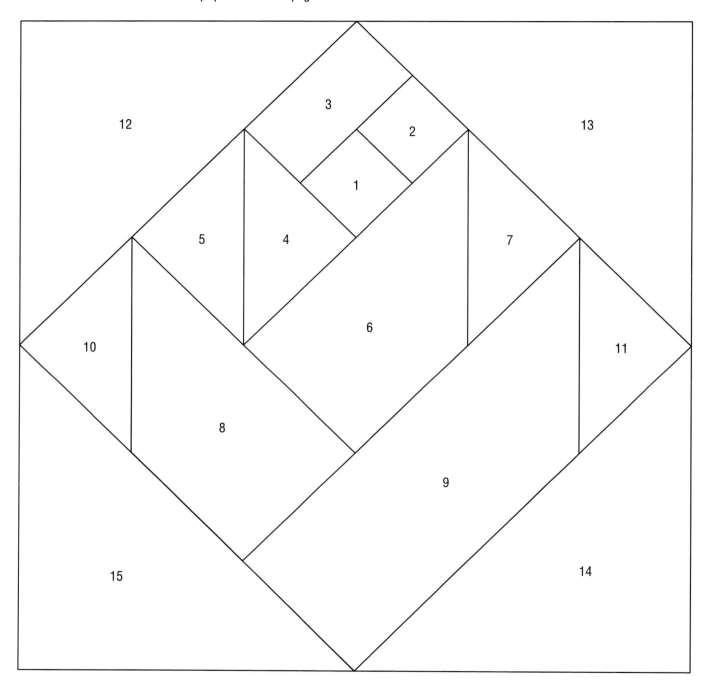

Block and Quilt Design Possibilities

Eliminating and Adding Seam Lines

The block designs presented in this book represent only a fraction of the possible block variations. You can sew them as presented or create additional block design variations by eliminating one or more seam lines. There are no patchwork police who will search you out if you don't piece all the sections of the blocks as they appear here. You can eliminate lines if you can continue the piecing sequence with no consequence. The illustration below shows how to make several variations of the same block by eliminating seam lines.

Block variations—Eliminating seams can yield
different design possibilities.

As you plan your quilt projects, using these block designs, remember to consider the block-variation possibilities.

You can also add seam lines to create block-design variations. You can do this if the piecing sequence can continue across the added lines or if the added seam line is the last seam. Additional seam lines can serve to make a design more intricate or can actually simplify a block.

You can eliminate merging seams in the corner of a block by adding a seam across the corner. This is a helpful option if you plan to piece two or four blocks in rotation. Measure the same distance from the corner and connect the line. Voila! The merging corner seams are no more.

Block designs that benefit from an additional last seam line across the corner have a dotted line to indicate the last seam variation.

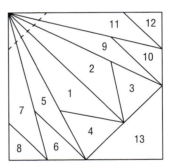

Value Options

Changing the value of the fabric in each area of the design can further increase the design possibilities. Value is the amount of lightness or darkness; a black-and-white photograph shows only values. The same line drawing can offer a variety of design possibilities, depending upon the placement of values. The following block looks very different when you change the values.

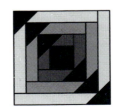

The same block with different value placement

Experiment with value changes by coloring in sections of the block-front drawings with a lead pencil in light, medium, and dark shadings to discover other design possibilities. Once you have decided on the values, use colored pencils to experiment with color in the design.

Fabric Choices

There are so many fabric possibilities. You can use a group of coordinated fabrics to complete a project of the same block design or a combination of several block designs. Or, select a multicolor print for the main fabric in a block or project and add a group of fabrics that contain the same colors found in the print.

The miniature blocks offer a wonderful opportunity to use all those scraps you have been saving. Place scraps randomly, using only the value in the scraps to create interesting designs. Separate scraps by color and use the same color scraps in one section of a block and different color scraps in another section. You can also use scraps in a random fashion without regard to value or color.

Incorporate novelty-type fabrics, such as silks and lamé, into the designs. Lamé flames in the Candle block add excitement. Since the paper helps to stabilize the pieces and a short stitch is used, you can use many fabrics that might not otherwise be used in patchwork.

Small-scale prints fit the proportions of miniature blocks, while large-scale prints provide splashes of color. You must take great care when using striped or checked fabrics. When sewing from the marked side of the block, it's difficult to see if you are sewing along a straight line on a striped or checked fabric. For this reason, you may want to avoid these types of fabrics or turn them so the lines will not run parallel to the seam line. When using random-grain piecing, select tiny-scale print fabrics instead of solid fabrics so the changes in grain lines will not be so obvious. If you are using tracing paper, you can easily center a particular design, such as a flower, inside the lines of the first piece for a special touch.

Block Placement

When blocks are set straight, some blocks have a central, vertical, and/or horizontal design, and others have a diagonal design that radiates from a corner. You can place straight-set blocks that have a diagonal design in pairs or in sets of four and rotate them to create new and interesting designs. Don't overlook this possibility for creating striking, dramatic 8" blocks from 4" block designs.

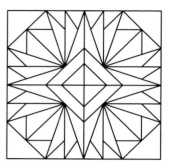

Design created by putting
four geometric blocks together

Try combining nine 4" blocks to create a 12" sampler patchwork square.

Quilt Layouts

It is now time to put all the pieces together. Make a quilt layout work sheet to try the block-front drawings in different positions and color schemes. On graph paper, draw a grid of 1" squares in a straight set or in a diagonal set, in the size you intend to make. Each square represents one block. Photocopy the grid layout for a ready supply of work sheets.

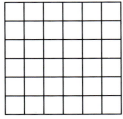 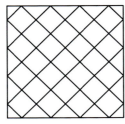

Straight set   Diagonal set

Begin by selecting a group of blocks and cut out photocopies of the block-front drawings. Move them around on the layout work sheet in different positions and rotations until you achieve a pleasing design. Consider using some of the simpler geometric blocks as alternate blocks between some of the more complicated blocks. These blocks offer interesting opportunities for interaction and provide areas to showcase hand quilting. The quilt does not have to contain only little pieces; separate the blocks with plain blocks, lattice strips, or border strips. These areas will not only enlarge the size of the quilt but will offer more opportunities for pretty quilting.

It is not necessary to have all the blocks appear to be the same size in the quilt project. For example, combine four 4" blocks to create an 8" block design. If the center portion of the quilt is comprised of four 8" block-design units, add a border containing 4" pieced blocks in the corner; then continue with 8" block-design units.

An example of a quilt layout that combines both 4" and 8" block-design units

When you have finalized a design, glue the blocks in place and make several photocopies of your quilt layout. Now use colored pencils to experiment with different color schemes. Don't forget to note the color on the unmarked side of your full-size block designs to correspond with the block-front drawings of the quilt design.

If a diagonal setting is chosen, you may want to include a half or quarter of a block on the edges or the corners. You can do this easily by drawing one diagonal line through the full-size pattern for half-square blocks and two diagonal lines for quarter-square blocks, then cutting the block into triangles. Piece the triangle patterns in sequence. Skip numbers that do not appear in that portion of the block. After the triangular block is pieced, trim the edge ¼" from the outside finished seam lines.

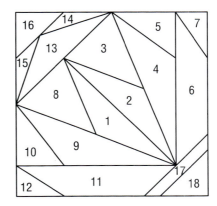

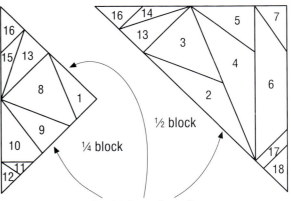

Cut ¼" from these lines to add seam allowance.

Project Size

To determine the size of a straight-set quilt layout, multiply the number of blocks vertically and horizontally times the size of the block chosen. For example, six blocks that are each 4" square will make a 24" project without borders. Six blocks that are each 6" square will make a project that is 36" without borders.

For diagonal-set quilt layouts, multiply the size of the block times 1.4142 to arrive at the diagonal measurement of the block. For example, a 4" block set on the diagonal has a 5⅝" diagonal measurement. Multiply this number times the number of blocks vertically and horizontally in the quilt to determine the quilt size without borders.

Use half-square triangles (straight grain on the short side) for corner triangles by cutting a square once diagonally. Determine the finished size of the short edge of the triangle; add ⅞" to this figure and cut a square that size.

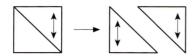

Half-square triangles
for corners

Use quarter-square triangles (straight grain on the long side) for side triangles by cutting a square twice diagonally. Determine the finished size of the long side of the triangle, then add 1¼" and cut a square that size.

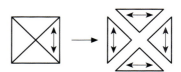

Quarter-square
triangles for sides

The following chart indicates the finished diagonal size of a variety of finished block sizes and the size squares to cut for the corner and side triangles.

Finished Block Size	Diagonal Size	Corner Triangles	Side Triangles
3"	4¼"	3 "	5½"
4"	5⅝"	3¾"	6⅞"
5"	7⅛"	4½"	8⅜"
6"	8½"	5⅛"	9¾"
7"	9⅞"	5⅞"	11⅛"
8"	11⅜"	6⅝"	12⅝"

Quilts

As I worked with these blocks in different quilt settings, I was amazed and delighted with the variety of quilt-design possibilities. Knowing that there would be many more designs when seen from another's perspective, I asked several of my friends to select blocks and create a quilt for this book. With the exception of Pam Ludwig, this was a new experience and these are their first quilts made using this method. I think they did a wonderful job, and they all admitted that machine paper piecing was fun.

The Quilt Plan indicates the block layout and borders. Make photocopies of the quilt plan so you can experiment with different color schemes. You can refer to the color photograph of the quilt or create a quilt in your own color combinations.

Each block design and color combination is assigned a letter. When a variation of a block design is used, the appropriate seam line(s) are eliminated or added to the design. See "Eliminating and Adding Seam Lines" on page 61.

The Block Placement Guide indicates the placement of each block design and various color variations in the sample quilt.

A	C	E	D	C	A
C	F	G	G	F	C
D	G	A	B	G	E
E	G	B	A	G	D
C	F	G	G	F	C
A	C	D	E	C	A

Block Placement Guide

The size of the blocks and borders used in the samples are also provided; however, you can complete these projects in a variety of sizes by changing the size of the blocks or the borders. You can use a 4" block design in place of 5", 6", and 7" blocks to make a smaller version of the same quilt.

You will find 7" block designs provided for the Tulips quilt (pages 59–60) and for the Not Exactly Amish quilt (page 58). Enlarging a 4" design to a 7" design requires making an enlargement from an enlargement, which is not recommended. See "Enlarging and Reducing Block Designs" on page 5.

Yardage

The yardage estimates for the sample quilts have been calculated generously to allow for oversize cutting of the pieces. When a small amount of fabric is used in one or two places in the quilt, a piece of fabric is given in inches. When small amounts of the same fabric are used several times in the quilt, a ⅛-yard minimum is given.

Cut larger pieces of fabric for borders, lattices, cornerstones, and bindings first; then use the remainder of the fabric to piece the blocks. There is sufficient yardage to add a few inches to the length of the borders just in case your quilt "grows" a bit during the piecing process. Fabric for binding has been calculated, using 2"-wide strips cut across the width of the fabric (crosswise grain) unless otherwise noted.

Floral Medallion

A	C	E	D	C	A
C	F	G	G	F	C
D	G	A	B	G	E
E	G	B	A	G	D
C	F	G	G	F	C
A	C	D	E	C	A

Color photo on page 84

Finished Block Size: 4"
Finished Inner Border: 1"
Finished Outer Border: 3½"
Finished Quilt Size: 33" x 33"

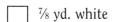 ⅞ yd. white

1 yd. dark green for blocks, outer border, and binding

¼ yd. medium green

⅓ yd. light green

¼ yd. dark red

⅓ yd. medium red for blocks and inner border

⅛ yd. pink

1 yd. for backing

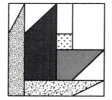

F2   A
Make 6

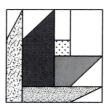

F2   B
Make 2

F7   C
Make 8

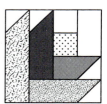

F3   D
Make 4

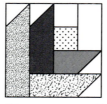

F3   E
Make 4

F4 variation   F
Make 4

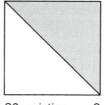

G3 variation   G
Make 8

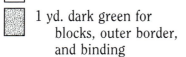

Little House in the Big Pines

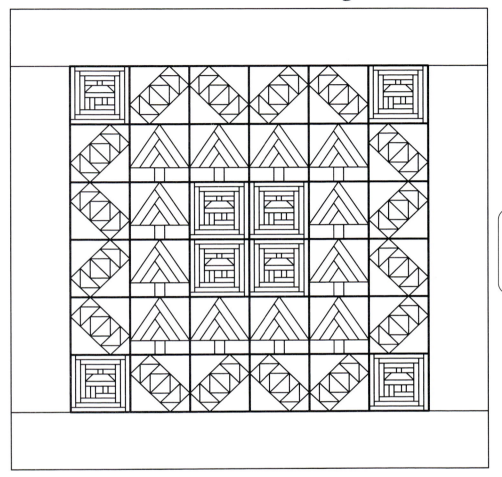

B	F	F	F	F	A
F	E	E	E	E	F
F	E	A	B	E	F
F	E	D	C	E	F
F	E	E	E	E	F
C	F	F	F	F	D

Color photo on page 83
Finished Block Size: 6"
Finished Border: 4"
Finished Quilt Size: 44" x 44"

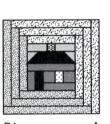

P1   A
Make 2

P1   B
Make 2

P1   C
Make 2

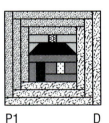

P1   D
Make 2

T1   E
Make 12

G2   F
Make 16

- 1⅝ yds. light blue
- 1 yd. assorted medium and dark green scraps
- 1 yd. assorted medium and dark blue scraps
- ⅛ yd. red for house
- ⅛ yd. brown for tree trunk
- ⅛ yd. blue for sky
- 1½" x 12" piece of dark red for chimney
- 1½" x 12" piece of yellow for house window
- ⅛ yd. black for house roof and door
- 1⅓ yds. blue for border and binding cut from lengthwise grain of fabric
- 2⅔ yds. for backing

Spring Baskets

A	A	E	E	A	A
A	F	D	C	F	A
E	C	B	B	D	E
E	D	B	B	C	E
A	F	C	D	F	A
A	A	E	E	A	A

Color photo on page 85

Finished Block Size: 6"
Finished Border: 5"
Finished Quilt Size: 46" x 46"

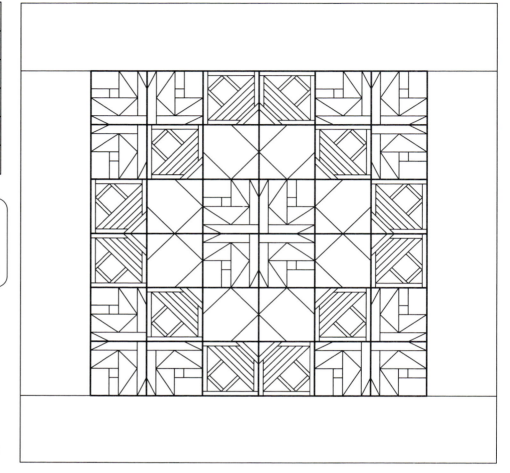

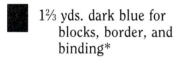 1⅔ yds. dark blue for blocks, border, and binding*

⅝ yd. blue-on-blue print

½ yd. blue paisley

¼ yd. solid blue

¼ yd. light blue

⅛ yd. blue-green

⅛ yd. red

¼ yd. light green

¼ yd. dark green

1⅞ yds. white

2¾ yds. for backing

Cut border and binding from lengthwise grain of fabric.

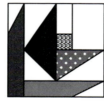

F1   A
Make 12

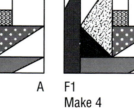

F1   B
Make 4

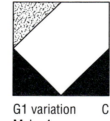

G1 variation   C
Make 4

G1 variation   D
Make 4

B1   E
Make 8

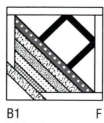

B1   F
Make 4

Lovable Cats

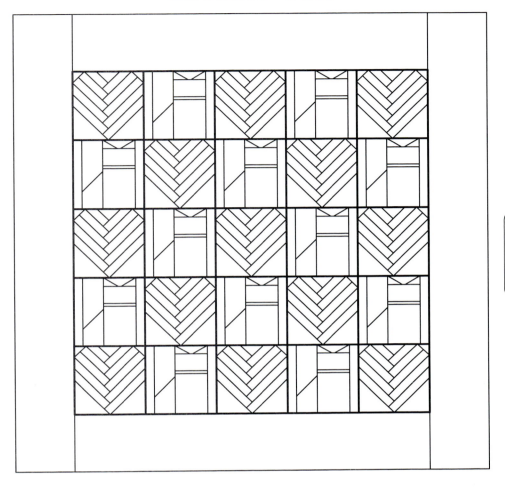

A	B	A	B	A
B	A	B	A	B
A	B	A	B	A
B	A	B	A	B
A	B	A	B	A

Color photo on page 87
Finished Block Size: 6"
Finished Border: 5"
Finished Quilt Size: 40" x 40"

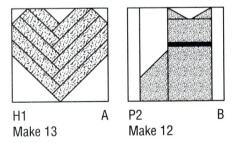

H1   A
Make 13

P2   B
Make 12

¾ yd. background

1 yd. total of multicolored scraps

12 different 4½" x 12" pieces for cats

⅛ yd. lamé or "glitzy" knit fabric for cat collars

1 yd. for border and binding

1¼ yds. for backing

Petite Baskets

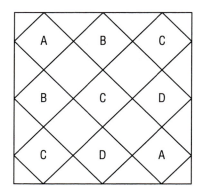

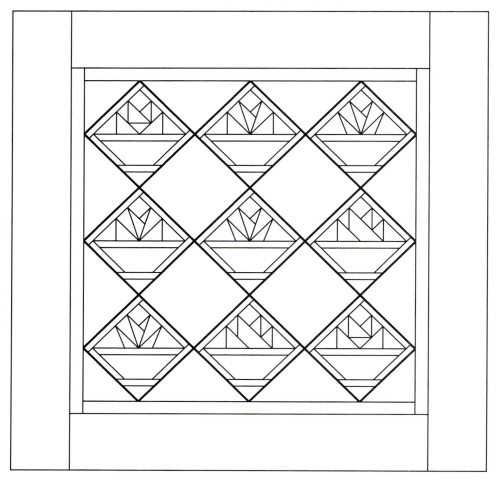

Color photo on page 86

Finished Block Size: 4"
Finished Inner Border: ¾"
Finished Outer Border: 3"
Finished Quilt Size:
24⅜" x 24⅜"

☐ ¾ yd. background

▨ ⅝ yd. floral for baskets
and outer border

▨ ¼ yd. light green

▪ ⅛ yd. medium green

▨ 4" square dark yellow

▨ 4" square medium yellow

▨ 4" square dark purple

▨ 4" square medium purple

▨ ⅓ yd. dark pink for
baskets, inner
border, and binding

▨ 4" square medium pink

▨ 4" square dark blue

▨ 4" square medium blue

¾ yd. for backing

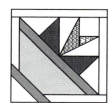

B3   A
Make 2

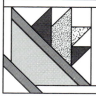

B5   B
Make 2

B6   C
Make 3

B4   D
Make 2

I'd Rather Be in Santa Fe

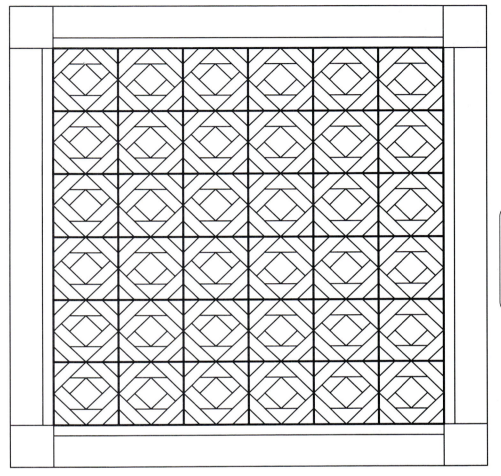

A	A	B	B	A	A
A	A	B	B	A	A
A	A	B	B	A	A
A	A	B	B	A	A
A	A	B	B	A	A
A	A	B	B	A	A

Color photo on page 90

Finished Block Size: 6"
Finished Inner Border: 1"
Finished Outer Border: 3"
Finished Quilt Size: 44" x 44"

G7   A
Make 24

G7   B
Make 12

 2 yds. dark red for blocks, outer border, and binding

 ⅝ yd. pink

1 yd. light blue for blocks, inner border, and corner squares

⅞ yd. light teal

 ⅝ yd. medium teal

 ⅓ yd. dark teal

2¾ yds. for backing

Springtime Anytime

B	C	A	C	B
C	D	C	D	C
A	C	A	C	A
C	D	C	D	C
B	C	A	C	B

Color photo on page 87

Finished Block Size: 6"
Finished Inner Border: 1"
Finished Outer Border: 4"
Finished Quilt Size: 40" x 40"

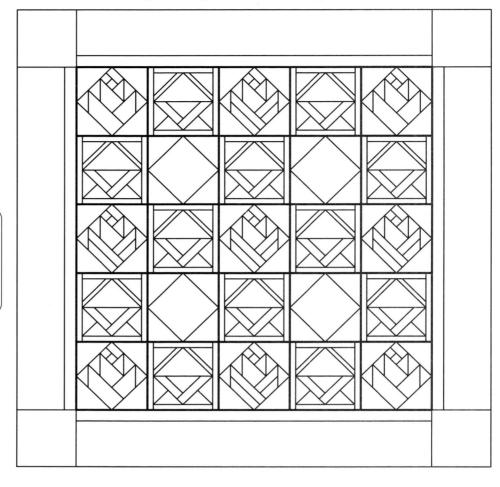

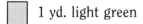 1 yd. light green

⬜ ⅝ yd. white

▦ ⅛ yd. light coral

▦ ⅓ yd. medium coral for blocks, inner border, and corner blocks

▦ ⅛ yd. dark coral

▦ ⅓ yd. medium green

⬛ 1½ yds. dark green for blocks, outer border, and binding

1¼ yds. for backing

F4   A
Make 5

F4 variation   B
Make 4

B2   C
Make 12

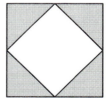

G1 variation   D
Make 4

Home Is Where the Heart Is

A	B	C	D
E	F	G	H
H	G	H	C
D	E	B	A

Color photo on page 83

Finished Block Size: 4"
Finished Inner Border: 2"
Finished Outer Border: 2"
Finished Quilt Size: 24" x 24"

⅓ yd. total assorted red scraps

⅓ yd. white

⅜ yd. total assorted green scraps

⅛ yd. total assorted brown scraps

⅓ yd. multicolored print for blocks and inner border

⅛ yd. total assorted light scraps

½ yd. red for outer border and binding

¾ yd. for backing

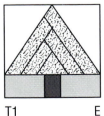

H2   A
Make 2

P3   B
Make 2

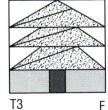

T2   C
Make 2

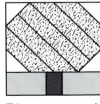

H3   D
Make 2

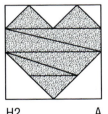

T1   E
Make 2

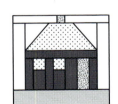

T3   F
Make 1

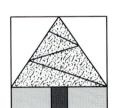

P4 variation   G
Make 2

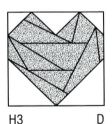

T4   H
Make 3

Tulips

Color photo on page 86

Finished Block Sizes: 3", 7"
Finished Lattice: 3"
Finished Border: 4½"
Finished Quilt Size: 42" x 42"

Grid layout (top left):

B		B		B		B
	A		C		A	
B		B		B		B
	C		A		C	
B		B		B		B
	A		C		A	
B		B		B		B

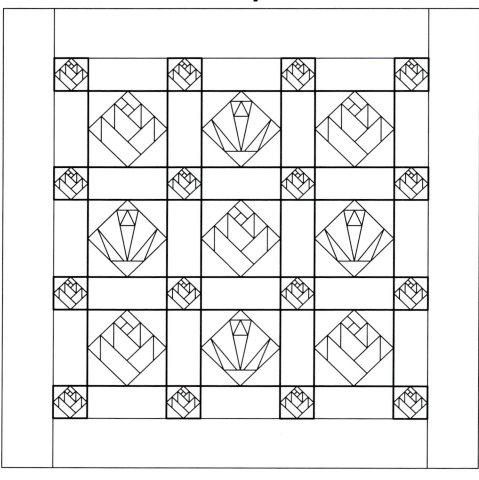

1¼ yds. white for blocks and lattice

⅛ yd. light pink

⅓ yd. medium pink

⅛ yd. dark pink

⅛ yd. yellow

1⅝ yds. medium green for blocks and border*

¾ yd. dark green for blocks and binding

2⅝ yds. for backing

Cut border from lengthwise grain of fabric.

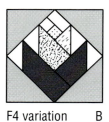

F4 variation   A
Make 5
7" size

F4 variation   B
Make 16
3" size

F5 variation   C
Make 4
7" size

Bird of Paradise

A	B	C	C	B	A
B	D	E	E	D	B
C	E	A	A	E	C
C	E	A	A	E	C
B	D	E	E	D	B
A	B	C	C	B	A

Color photo on page 85

Finished Block Size: 6"
Finished Inner Border: 1"
Finished Outer Border: 2¼"
Finished Quilt Size:
42½" x 42½"

F6 variation   A
Make 8

F8   B
Make 8

F7   C
Make 8

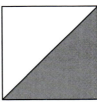

G3 variation   D
Make 4

G3 variation   E
Make 8

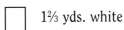

1⅔ yds. white

⅞ yd. magenta for blocks
and inner border

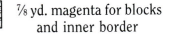

1¼ yds. dark magenta for
blocks, outer border,
and binding*

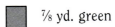

⅞ yd. green

⅜ yd. dark green

2½ yds. for backing

*Cut outer border and binding
from lengthwise grain of
fabric.*

Fathom

Color photo on page 90

Finished Block Size: 6"
Finished Border: 4"
Finished Quilt Size: 38" x 38"

A	A	C	C	A
B	D	B	E	F
G	G	G	G	G
H	I	H	I	H
J	K	K	K	J

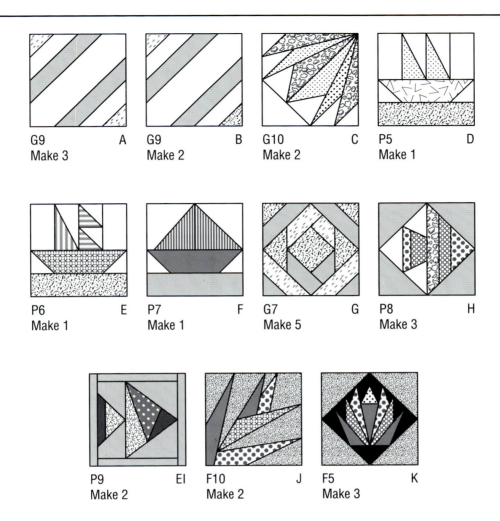

G9   A
Make 3

G9   B
Make 2

G10   C
Make 2

P5   D
Make 1

P6   E
Make 1

P7   F
Make 1

G7   G
Make 5

P8   H
Make 3

P9   EI
Make 2

F10   J
Make 2

F5   K
Make 3

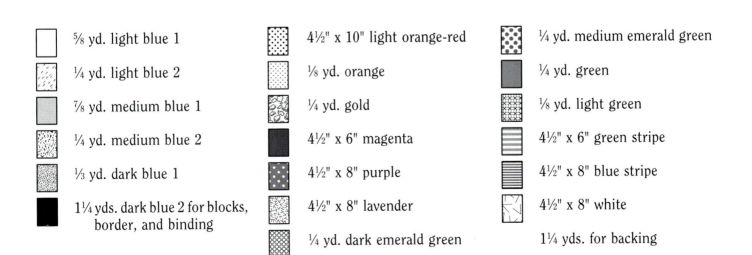

⅝ yd. light blue 1

¼ yd. light blue 2

⅞ yd. medium blue 1

¼ yd. medium blue 2

⅓ yd. dark blue 1

1¼ yds. dark blue 2 for blocks, border, and binding

4½" x 10" light orange-red

⅛ yd. orange

¼ yd. gold

4½" x 6" magenta

4½" x 8" purple

4½" x 8" lavender

¼ yd. dark emerald green

¼ yd. medium emerald green

¼ yd. green

⅛ yd. light green

4½" x 6" green stripe

4½" x 8" blue stripe

4½" x 8" white

1¼ yds. for backing

Hearts a Flutter

A	C	C	B
C	B	A	C
C	A	B	C
B	C	C	A

Color photo on page 88

Finished Block Size: 5"
Finished Inner Border: 1"
Finished Outer Border: 4"
Finished Quilt Size: 30" x 30"

 1⅜ yds. navy for blocks, outer border, and binding

 ⅜ yd. total assorted light red and pink scraps

 ¼ yd. total assorted medium red scraps

¼ yd. red for inner border

1 yd. for backing

H4   A
Make 4

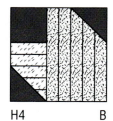

H4   B
Make 4

G6   C
Make 8

Not Exactly Amish

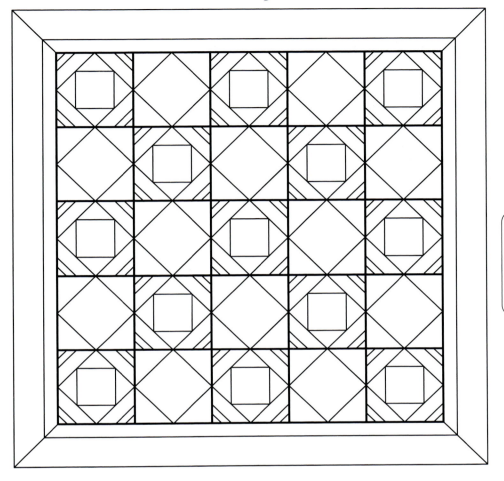

A	B	A	B	A
B	A	B	A	B
A	B	A	B	A
B	A	B	A	B
A	B	A	B	A

Color photo on page 89

Finished Block Size: 7"
Finished Inner Border: 1¼"
Finished Outer Border: 2¾"
Finished Quilt Size: 43" x 43"

G8
Make 13

A

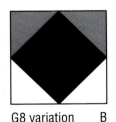

G8 variation
Make 12

B

□ ¾ yd. light blue

▨ ⅓ yd. medium blue

▨ 2 yds. dark blue for
     blocks, outer border,
     and binding*

▨ ⅓ yd. red

▨ ¼ yd. dark red

■ 1 yd. black for blocks
     and inner border

2⅝ yds. for backing

*Cut outer border and binding
from lengthwise grain of
fabric.*

Our Amish Friendship Garden

A	C	B	B	C	A
C	B	C	C	B	C
B	C	A	A	C	B
B	C	A	A	C	B
C	B	C	C	B	C
A	C	B	B	C	A

Color photo on page 89

Finished Block Size: 6"
Finished Border: 8"
Finished Quilt Size: 52" x 52"

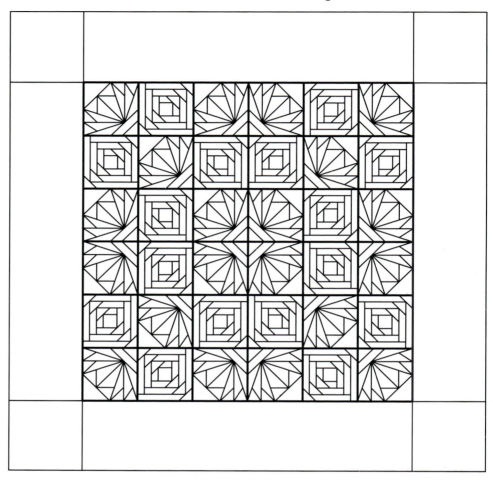

 2 yds. black for blocks, corner squares, and binding

 1⅞ yds. royal blue for blocks and border*

 ¾ yd. medium purple

 1 yd. dark purple

 ⅔ yd. light blue

 1 yd. light pink

 ¼ yd. lavender

3⅛ yds. for backing

Cut border from lengthwise grain of fabric.

G5
Make 8   A

G5
Make 12   B

G4
Make 16   C

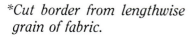

Woven Stars

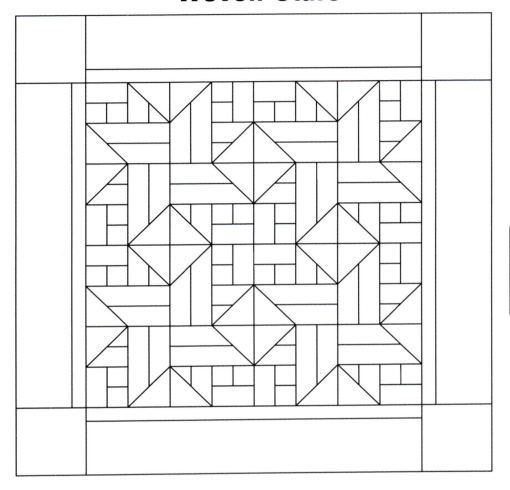

B	A	B	A
A	B	A	B
B	A	B	A
A	B	A	B

Color photo on page 88

Finished Block Size: 6"
Finished Inner Border: 1"
Finished Outer Border: 4"
Finished Quilt Size: 34" x 34"

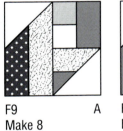

F9
Make 8

A

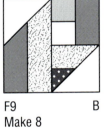

F9
Make 8

B

⅞ yd. dark pink for blocks and outer border

⅛ yd. light blue

½ yd. light pink

⅓ yd. medium blue

¾ yd. navy blue for blocks, inner border, corner squares, and binding

1⅛ yds. for backing

Plum Elegant

A A | | A A | | A A
A B D | | | D B A
| D D D D D D |
A | D C C D | | A
A | D C C D | | A
| D D D D D D |
A B D | | | D B A
A A | | A A | | A A

Color photo on page 84

Finished Block Size: 5"
Finished Border: 5"
Finished Quilt Size: 50" x 50"

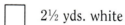 2½ yds. white

2⁄3 yd. light floral

¼ yd. medium plum

1⅜ yds. deep plum for blocks and binding

1¾ yds. dark green for blocks and border*

3 yds. for backing

F6 variation   A
Make 20

F6 variation   B
Make 4

F6 variation   C
Make 4

F7   D
Make 20

*Cut border from lengthwise grain of fabric.

Gallery of Quilts

Home Is Where the Heart Is *by Doreen C. Burbank, 1993, Windham, New Hampshire, 24" x 24". The random placement of the trees, hearts, and houses creates an interesting and varied village quilt. These little blocks offered Doreen lots of opportunity to use her scrap basket while creating a delightful quilt.*

Little House in the Big Pines *by Carol Doak, 1993, Windham, New Hampshire, 44" x 44". Three different blocks—a Tree block, a Picture block, and a Geometric block—were used to create this medallion scrap quilt. Randomly placed shades of green appear in the trees and shades of blue in the flying-geese border, then both of these colors show up in the Little House blocks in four different color schemes.*

Plum Elegant *by Pamela Ludwig, 1993, Windham, New Hampshire, 50" x 50". Pam received the prize for using the most blocks in her quilt—a total of 64. She created this delicate quilt design by using two different Flower block variations of the same design, with a color change in one of the variations, and a third Flower block. The addition of plain blocks allowed Pam to showcase her pretty quilting, which resulted in an elegant medallion-style quilt with the illusion of circular patterns in the middle.*

Floral Medallion *by Carol Doak, 1993, Windham, New Hampshire, 33" x 33". This dramatic medallion quilt uses four different floral designs to set the theme and a variation of a Geometric design to create the star in the middle. The angles created by block F7 provide a wonderful circular effect.*

Spring Baskets *by Carol Doak, 1993, Windham, New Hampshire, 46" x 46". This medallion quilt utilizes one Basket block, one Flower block, and one Geometric block variation. Keeping the same color strips in the body of the baskets creates the effect of a diamond within a square. Changing the color placement in the base of the top and side baskets creates a handle for yet another little basket radiating from the center.*

Bird of Paradise *by Nancy Bell, 1993, Hollis, New Hampshire, 42½" x 42½". Nancy used two Flower blocks, a variation of a Flower block, and a variation of a Geometric block to create this graphic medallion quilt. Nancy chose the added seam variation across the corner of block F6 to reduce the number of merging seams. The resulting center diagonal square was perfect to accentuate the larger diagonal square in the center of the quilt, where she was able to showcase her quilting.*

Petite Baskets *by Carol Doak, 1993, Windham, New Hampshire, 24⅜" x 24⅜". This diagonally set quilt is made up of four different Basket blocks alternated with solid blocks. The pretty floral pastel fabric used in the baskets and the border set the theme and was the basis for selecting the flower colors. The alternating solid blocks offer the opportunity to include pretty hand-quilted designs. This delicate little quilt with only nine pieced blocks works up very quickly!*

Tulips *by Moira Clegg, 1993, Windham, New Hampshire, 42" x 42". Moira used two Flower block variations to create this soft and restful quilt. A miniature Tulip block, repeated in the same color combination, appears in the cornerstones of the wide white lattice.*

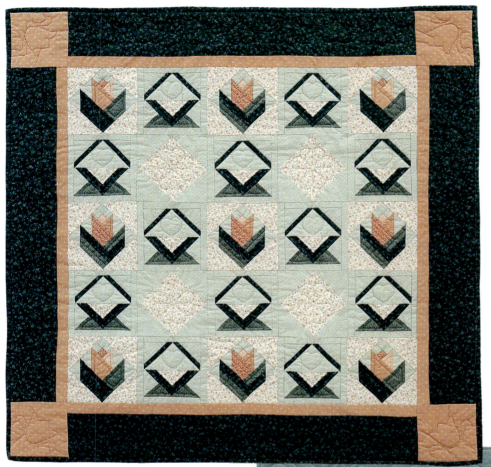

Springtime Anytime *by Beth Meek, 1993, Windham, New Hampshire, 40" x 40". Beth used a Flower block and a variation of the same block in combination with a Basket design to create this delicate quilt. The corner triangles in the Flower blocks create a variation in the background fabric, which adds yet another dimension to this quilt. The Geometric block variation offers opportunity for pretty hand quilting. As Beth worked on her quilt through three major New Hampshire snowstorms, she named her quilt for the feeling of springtime it evoked.*

Lovable Cats *by Carol Doak, 1993, Windham, New Hampshire, 40" x 40". This alternating-block quilt utilizes one Heart block and one Picture block. The number of strips in the Heart block provides a great place to use up lots of fabric scraps. The Cat blocks work up very quickly with only ten pieces. A different fabric is used in each cat to carry the scrap theme. A "glitzy" metallic knit fabric is used for the cat collars in order to dress them up just a bit.*

Woven Stars *by Mary Kay Sieve, 1993, Windham, New Hampshire, 34" x 34". Mary Kay used just one floral block pattern to create this "star" quilt. A slight color change in the block creates the illusion that the sections of the star are woven together.*

Hearts a Flutter *by Margaret Forand, 1993, Sutton Mills, New Hampshire, 30" x 30". Peggy used a Heart block in two color combinations of red and pink scraps to create the woven center design of her quilt. She used the lighter shade of scraps in the flying-geese Geometric blocks, which surround the center, to create a graphic frame. The navy blue background really sets off all the red and pink scraps. The wider border offers a place for the pretty hand-quilted heart design.*

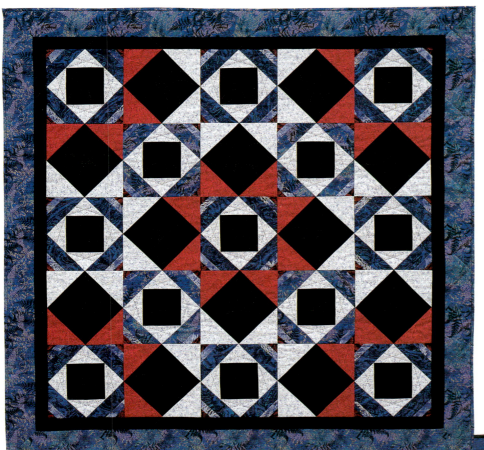

Not Exactly Amish *by Shawn Walker Levy, 1993, Trumbauersville, Pennsylvania, 43" x 43". Shawn used the same color combinations in just one Geometric block and a variation of the same block to create this colorful quilt that looks much more complicated than it is. The rotation of the block variation creates the center star and the corner accents. The black background fabric makes the colors come alive and aids in the three-dimensional illusion.*

Our Amish Friendship Garden *by Sherry Reis, 1993, Worthington, Ohio, 52" x 52". Sherry created this wonderful design by combining just two Geometric blocks. She used the same color combination in all G4 blocks, and two color combinations in the G5 blocks, to accentuate the diamond shape created by rotating these blocks around the center. Amish colors carry the theme. The wide border offered Sherry the opportunity to add beautiful hand quilting.*

Fathom *by Virginia L. Guaraldi, 1993, Londonderry, New Hampshire, 38" x 38". Ginny received the prize for using the greatest number of different blocks in her quilt. She combined eleven different blocks to create this whimsical, nautical summertime quilt. With the exception of the G9 block, she completed all the blocks in the same fabric combinations. The shades of blue fabric in this quilt deepen as they progress from the sky to the bottom of the sea. Ginny celebrates the individual by letting one of the fish swim in the opposite direction.*

I'd Rather Be in Santa Fe *by Carolyn K. Inglis, 1993, Hudson, New Hampshire, 44" x 44". Carolyn used just one block design in two color combinations to achieve this intricate southwestern design.*

Quilt Finishing

Joining Blocks

Arrange blocks as shown in the block placement guide for the quilt you are making. To join blocks, place blocks right sides together, matching the outer lines on the marked block. Place pins through the lines of both blocks and stitch along the marked line of the block. I machine baste important matching points before sewing the seam to check for a good match. Once the seam is machine basted, you can open it for a quick check to make sure the seams align correctly. If they do, proceed to sew the seam. If they don't quite match, remove the machine basting and try again. Basting at these crucial matching points also secures the area so it won't shift while sewing. Machine basting takes just a few minutes but eliminates a lot of frustration.

 TIP: Place a block with points at the outside edge facing up as you sew the seam. This way, you will be sure you are sewing across the point and not through it. If both blocks have points, have faith!

Sew blocks together in horizontal rows and press the seams in opposite directions from row to row. Pressing in this manner will lock the seams into a good match. Sew the rows together, making sure to match the seams between each block.

 TIP: If the outside edges of your blocks are mostly one fabric color, change the thread to match.

Adding Borders

The quilts in this book are completed with both straight-cut corners and mitered corners.

Straight-Cut Corners

1. Measure the length of the quilt top at the center, from raw edge to raw edge, and cut two border strips to that measurement. Mark the center of the

border strips and the sides of the quilt top; join the borders to the sides, matching center marks and edges and easing as necessary. Press the seams toward the borders.

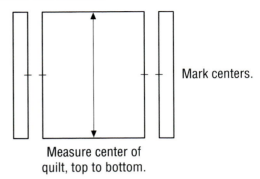

Measure center of quilt, top to bottom.

Mark centers.

2. Measure the width of the quilt top through the center, from raw edge to raw edge, including the border pieces just added; cut two border strips to that measurement. Mark the centers of the border strips and the top and bottom of the quilt top; join the border strips to the top and bottom edges, matching centers and ends and easing as necessary. Press the seams toward the borders.

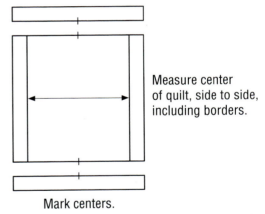

Measure center of quilt, side to side, including borders.

Mark centers.

If desired, you may add the top and bottom border strips first, then the sides.

Borders with Cornerstones

1. Measure for all four border strips before attaching side borders as described for borders with straight-cut corners. Sew the border strips to opposite sides of the quilt top first; press the seams toward the borders.

 NOTE: If your quilt has multiple borders, sew the individual strips together and treat as one unit before adding cornerstones.

2. Attach the cornerstones to the top and bottom strips and press the seams toward the border strips; then sew these strips to the top and bottom edges of the quilt top.

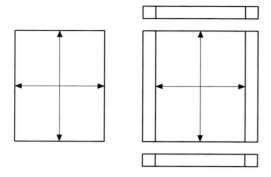

Mitered Corners

1. First estimate the finished outside dimensions of your quilt, including borders. Border strips should be cut to this length and width, plus at least ½" for seam allowances; 2"–3" is even better to give yourself some leeway.

 NOTE: If your quilt has multiple borders, sew the individual strips together and treat the resulting unit as a single piece for mitering.

2. Mark the centers of the quilt edges and the centers of the border strips. Stitch all four borders to the quilt top with a ¼"-wide seam, matching centers; the border strip should extend the same distance at each end of the quilt. Start and stop your stitching ¼" from the corners of the quilt top; press the seams toward the borders.

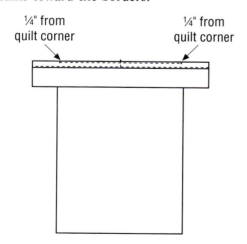

¼" from quilt corner   ¼" from quilt corner

3. Remove the paper from the wrong side of the blocks. See below.

4. Lay the first corner you are going to miter on the ironing board. Fold one of the border units under, at a 45° angle. Work with the fold until seams meet; pin at the fold, then check to see that the outside corner is square and that there is no extra fullness at the edges. When everything is straight and square, press the fold. Pin the borders together to prevent them from shifting.

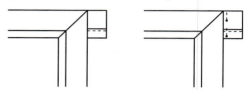

5. Fold the center section of the quilt diagonally from corner to corner, right sides together, and align the long edges of the border strips. Draw a light pencil line on the crease created when you pressed the fold. Stitch on the pencil line; check to see that the miter is correct before trimming excess fabric. Press the seam open. Repeat these steps for the remaining three corners.

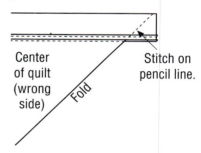

Center of quilt (wrong side)   Fold   Stitch on pencil line.

Removing the Paper and Pressing the Blocks

Remove the paper only after the completed blocks have been joined to other blocks or borders. Tracing paper is easier to remove than photocopy paper. A slight tug on the seam will loosen the paper from the stitching. A sewing stiletto is helpful in picking up the edge of the paper along the stitching line to lift and tear it away. Use a small pair of tweezers to remove pieces of paper left behind. Don't concern yourself with tiny pieces of paper. They will only add warmth to the quilt!

Once the paper has been removed, press the blocks gently with a dry iron in an up-and-down motion. Dragging a steam iron across the blocks will distort them.

Basting

Once the paper has been removed, you are ready to sandwich and baste the top. The sandwich consists of the backing, the batting, and the quilt top. There are many types of quilt batting available. Use a thin, low-loft batting for small wall quilts—they don't need to keep the wall warm. The low-loft batting also helps you to take smaller stitches in quilting the smaller-scale designs. Cut the backing and the batting 2"–3" larger than the quilt top all around.

1. Spread the backing, wrong side up, on a clean surface. Use masking tape or large binder clamps to anchor the backing to the table, being careful not to stretch it out of shape.
2. Spread and smooth the quilt batting over the backing, making sure it covers the entire backing.
3. Place the quilt top on top of the batting, right side up, smoothing out any wrinkles. Make sure the edges of the quilt top are parallel to the edges of the backing.
4. Beginning in the middle and working to the outside edges, make diagonal, vertical, and horizontal rows of basting stitches in a grid. An alternative method is pin basting with size 2, rustproof safety pins.

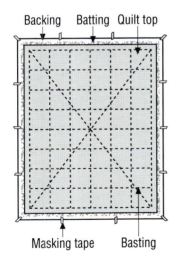

Backing   Batting   Quilt top

Masking tape   Basting

5. Bring the edge of the backing around to the front of the quilt top and baste in place in order to contain any exposed batting while quilting.

Quilting

These quilts can be hand quilted or machine quilted. If you prefer hand quilting, keep in mind that piecing tiny blocks with this method does not leave a large amount of single-layer fabric available for hand quilting, so plan accordingly. You might want to alternate solid squares and/or add plain fabric borders to showcase your hand quilting. On the other hand, small projects that utilize miniature blocks can be easily machine quilted.

Begin quilting the project in the middle and work toward the outside in a consistent fashion. It is similar to wall papering, when you smooth the bubbles out to the outside edge.

Binding

Once you have completed the quilting, it is time to bind the quilt. Prepare the quilt by removing the basting stitches and trimming the batting and backing even with the edge of the quilt top. Using a walking foot or an even-feed foot on your sewing machine, if available, sew a basting stitch around the perimeter approximately ⅛" from the edge. The even-feed foot aids in sewing all three layers smoothly. If you are adding a sleeve to hang your quilt project, you should baste it in place now. (See page 94.) Because the edges of wall quilts do not receive stress from handling, I prefer to use binding that has been cut on the straight grain. I use fabric strips cut on the bias when binding bed quilts because bias strips are stronger.

To make straight-grain binding:

1. Cut strips 2" wide across the width of the fabric (crosswise grain) and seam the ends at a 45° angle to make a strip long enough to go around the outside edges of the quilt, plus about 10"; trim excess fabric and press seams open.

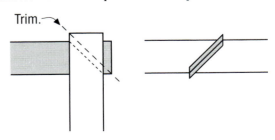

Trim.

2. Fold the strip in half lengthwise, wrong sides together, and press.

3. Place the binding on the front of the quilt, lining up the raw edges of the binding with the raw edges of the quilt. Using a walking foot, if possible, sew the binding to the quilt with a ¼"-wide seam; leave the first few inches of the binding loose so that you can join the beginning and ending of the binding strip later.

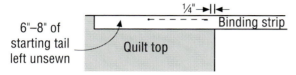

6"–8" of starting tail left unsewn

¼"→‖←

Binding strip

Quilt top

4. Stop stitching ¼" from the corner of the quilt and backstitch. Turn the quilt to sew the next edge. Fold the binding up and away from the quilt and then down, even with the next side. The straight fold should be even with the top edge of the quilt. Stitch from the edge to the next corner, stopping ¼" from the corner. Repeat for remaining corners.

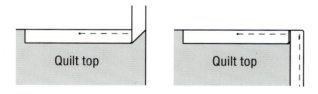

Quilt top

Quilt top

5. As you approach the beginning of the binding, stop and overlap the binding ½" from the start of the binding strip and trim excess. Open the folds of the two strips and sew the ends together with a ¼"-wide seam allowance. Return the seamed strip to the edge and finish the seam.

6. Fold binding to the back over the raw edges of the quilt. The folded edge of the binding should cover the machine-stitching line. Blindstitch the binding in place.

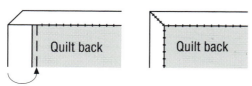

Quilt back

Quilt back

Adding a Sleeve

The preferred method for hanging a wall quilt is to slip a rod through a sleeve that has been sewn on the back of the quilt. You can use the same fabric as the backing so it will blend in, or simply use a piece of muslin.

1. Cut a strip of fabric as long as the width of the quilt; double the size of the rod plus ½". Hem both ends of the strip.

2. Fold the strip, wrong sides together, and pin the raw edges at the top of the quilt before you attach the binding. Baste in place ⅛" from the edge. Add the binding to the quilt as described on pages 93–94.

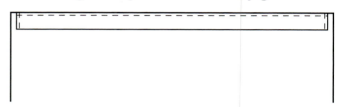

3. Blindstitch the folded edge of the sleeve to the back of the quilt.

Signing Your Work

The final touch to your quilt project is a label on the back. Don't leave future generations wondering about your quilt. The label can be as simple as writing on a piece of fabric with a permanent pen, or you may want to make one with elaborate hand embroidery or cross-stitch. Include your name and the date. You could also include the name of your quilt, the recipient's name if it is a gift, the name of your town and state, and any other information you would like to add.

About the Author . . .

Carol Doak is an award-winning quiltmaker, author, and teacher. She has made over 150 quilts since taking her first quiltmaking class in Worthington, Ohio, in 1979. Carol began teaching quiltmaking almost immediately and currently travels nationally to share her quiltmaking "Tricks of the Trade." She writes a regular column of the same title for *Quick and Easy Quilting* magazine. Her lighthearted approach and ability to teach have earned her high marks and positive comments from workshop participants nationwide.

Carol's Blue Ribbon quilts have been presented in several books, such as *Great American Quilts 1990* and *The Quilt Encyclopedia*. She has been featured in several national quilt magazines, and her quilts have appeared on the cover of *Quilter's Newsletter, Quilt World,* and *Quilting Today.*

Carol's first book, *Quiltmaker's Guide: Basics & Beyond,* was published in 1992. With her easy and inspiring teaching style, Carol sees her writing as a means to reach more quiltmakers.

Presently, Carol lives with her family in Windham, New Hampshire, where the long, cold winters offer her many opportunities to cozy under quilts in progress.

That Patchwork Place Publications and Products

BOOKS

Angle Antics by Mary Hickey
Animas Quilts by Jackie Robinson
Appliqué Borders: An Added Grace by Jeana Kimball
Baltimore Bouquets by Mimi Dietrich
Basket Garden by Mary Hickey
Biblical Blocks by Rosemary Makhan
Blockbuster Quilts by Margaret J. Miller
Calendar Quilts by Joan Hanson
Cathedral Window: A Fresh Look by Nancy J. Martin
Corners in the Cabin by Paulette Peters
Country Medallion Sampler by Carol Doak
Country Threads by Connie Tesene and Mary Tendall
Easy Machine Paper Piecing by Carol Doak
Even More by Trudie Hughes
Fantasy Flowers: Pieced Flowers for Quilters
    by Doreen Cronkite Burbank
Feathered Star Sampler by Marsha McCloskey
Fit To Be Tied by Judy Hopkins
Five- and Seven-Patch Blocks & Quilts for the ScrapSaver™
    by Judy Hopkins
Four-Patch Blocks & Quilts for the ScrapSaver™
    by Judy Hopkins
Go Wild with Quilts: 14 North American Birds and Animals
    by Margaret Rolfe
Handmade Quilts by Mimi Dietrich
Happy Endings—Finishing the Edges of Your Quilt
    by Mimi Dietrich
Holiday Happenings by Christal Carter
Home for Christmas by Nancy J. Martin and Sharon Stanley
In The Beginning by Sharon Evans Yenter
Jacket Jazz by Judy Murrah
Lessons in Machine Piecing by Marsha McCloskey
Little By Little: Quilts in Miniature by Mary Hickey
Little Quilts by Alice Berg, Sylvia Johnson, and
    Mary Ellen Von Holt
Lively Little Logs by Donna McConnell
Loving Stitches: A Guide to Fine Hand Quilting
    by Jeana Kimball
More Template-Free™ *Quiltmaking* by Trudie Hughes
Nifty Ninepatches by Carolann M. Palmer
Nine-Patch Blocks & Quilts for the ScrapSaver™
    by Judy Hopkins
Not Just Quilts by Jo Parrott
On to Square Two by Marsha McCloskey

Osage County Quilt Factory by Virginia Robertson
Painless Borders by Sally Schneider
A Perfect Match: A Guide to Precise Machine Piecing
    by Donna Lynn Thomas
Picture Perfect Patchwork by Naomi Norman
Piecemakers® *Country Store* by the Piecemakers
Pineapple Passion by Nancy Smith and Lynda Milligan
A Pioneer Doll and Her Quilts by Mary Hickey
Pioneer Storybook Quilts by Mary Hickey
*Quick & Easy Quiltmaking: 26 Projects Featuring Speedy
    Cutting and Piecing Methods* by Mary Hickey,
    Nancy J. Martin, Marsha McCloskey & Sara Nephew
Quilts for All Seasons: Year-Round Log Cabin Designs
    by Christal Carter
Quilts for Baby: Easy as A, B, C by Ursula Reikes
Quilts for Kids by Carolann M. Palmer
Quilts from Nature by Joan Colvin
Quilts to Share by Janet Kime
Red and Green: An Appliqué Tradition by Jeana Kimball
Red Wagon Originals by Gerry Kimmel and Linda Brannock
Rotary Riot: 40 Fast & Fabulous Quilts by Judy Hopkins
    and Nancy J. Martin
Rotary Roundup: 40 More Fast & Fabulous Quilts by Judy
    Hopkins and Nancy J. Martin
Samplings from the Sea by Rosemary Makhan
Scrap Happy by Sally Schneider
*Sensational Settings: Over 80 Ways to Arrange Your Quilt
    Blocks* by Joan Hanson
Sewing on the Line: Fast and Easy Foundation Piecing
    by Lesly-Claire Greenberg
Shortcuts: A Concise Guide to Rotary Cutting
    by Donna Lynn Thomas (metric version available)
Small Talk by Donna Lynn Thomas
Smoothstitch™ *Quilts: Easy Machine Appliqué*
    by Roxi Eppler
The Stitchin' Post by Jean Wells and Lawry Thorn
Strips That Sizzle by Margaret J. Miller
Tea Party Time: Romantic Quilts and Tasty Tidbits
    by Nancy J. Martin
Template-Free™ *Quiltmaking* by Trudie Hughes
Template-Free™ *Quilts and Borders* by Trudie Hughes
Template-Free® *Stars* by Jo Parrott
Watercolor Quilts by Pat Maixner Magaret and
    Donna Ingram Slusser
Women and Their Quilts by Nancyann Johanson Twelker

TOOLS

6" Bias Square®	Rotary Mate™
8" Bias Square®	Rotary Rule™
Metric Bias Square®	Ruby Beholder™
BiRangle™	ScrapSaver™
Pineapple Rule	

VIDEO

Shortcuts to America's Best-Loved Quilts

Many titles are available at your local quilt shop. For more information, send $2 for a color catalog to That Patchwork Place, Inc., PO Box 118, Bothell WA 98041-0118 USA.

☎ Call 1-800-426-3126 for the name and location of the quilt shop nearest you.